HOW COME
THEY'RE HAPPY
AND
I'M NOT?

The COMPLETE NATURAL MEDICINE PROGRAM
for HEALING DEPRESSION *for* GOOD

PETER BONGIORNO, ND, LAC

Conari Press

First published in 2012 by Conari Press
Red Wheel/Weiser, LLC
With offices at:
665 Third Street, Suite 400
San Francisco, CA 94107

ISBN: 978-1-57324-580-7

Cover design by Jim Warner
Cover photograph ©Radius/SuperStock
Interior by Maureen Forys, Happenstance Type-O-Rama

Figures 1, 3, and 4 first printed in Peter Bongiorno's Healing Depression:
Integrated Naturopathic and Conventional Treatments. CCNM Publishing,
2010. Reprinted with permission.

Printed in the United States of America

This book is dedicated to my patients who have been, by far, my greatest teachers, inspirations, and help in writing this work. It's an honor to work with courageous women and men every day who share their stories, fears, intelligence, and passion for life with me in hope. I thank you and all who are challenged by mood. I offer my most profound respect and admiration.

I co-dedicate this book to every researcher whose tireless lab work and clinical hours contributed to the information that made this book possible.

The best six doctors anywhere
And no one can deny it
Are sunshine, water, rest, and air
Exercise and diet.
These six will gladly you attend
If only you are willing
Your mind they'll ease
Your will they'll mend
And charge you not a shilling.

—Nursery rhyme, School Life, Vol IV, 1920

CONTENTS

PART III: Meds, Gender, and Seniors

ACKNOWLEDGMENTS

To my best friend, wife, and fellow naturopathic doctor, Pina, who did everything else there was to do so I could write.

I thank my parents, Peter and Patricia, for giving me every opportunity in life to follow my passions. To the Bongiornos, LoGiudices, Coppolas, and Zaccarias for their constant love.

Tremendous gratitude to Patricia Karpas and Mary Jane Ryan, who allowed this project to take substance and connect. To Caroline Pincus and everyone at Red Wheel/Weiser and Conari, who made my maiden voyage into the non-academic publishing world a kind and gentle learning experience.

. . . and to Sophia, my little rock star.

This book is strictly informational and is not intended as a substitute for medical advice. If you have a specific health concern or are experiencing any symptoms that scare or concern you, please contact a health care professional in your area and seek immediate medical help.

INTRODUCTION

A Short History of Depression

The goal of life is to make your heartbeat match the beat of the universe, to match your nature with Nature.

—JOSEPH CAMPBELL

On any given day, 18 million Americans are depressed. That's almost 10 percent of the population. And that doesn't even count the 3.3 million of you who are suffering from dysthymia (chronic low mood). Despite America's amazing health care system, by 2020 depression will be the second leading cause of burden and disability not only in America but also worldwide, second only to heart disease. It's also the leading cause of disease for women among high-, middle-, and low-income countries.

"THE BEST HEALTH CARE IN THE WORLD"?

I was speaking a bit tongue in cheek when I said "amazing health care system." I cannot tell you how many medical lectures I have been to in my almost twenty years of research, schooling, and clinical practice in which some doctor or administrator has claimed that our system in America is the "number one system in the world." I need to let you, and those speakers, in on a little fact: The World Health Organization looked closely at the efficacy of health care systems around the world and ranked the American system with other countries. Can you guess where we were ranked? Number one or two? In the top five? Nope, nope, and nope. Actually, we came up as number thirty-seven out of 191 countries, right between Costa Rica and Slovenia. And, to get that revered position, we outspend any other country per person by more than 250 percent—so we spend the most money to keep our thirty-seventh place. Further, it seems life expectancy is actually going down. In 2005, the *New England Journal of Medicine* announced that for the first time the new generation would not likely live as long as the previous one. Yikes. Why are we spending all this money in order to be living shorter lives?

In the spirit of balance, let me also make it clear that, as a naturopathic physician (please see more about naturopathic medicine in the resources section of this book), I am not anti-medical doctor and I am not antidrug. When modern medicine is used appropriately, it can save a life—no doubt. A quick story about me: When I was five years old, I had a benign tumor on one of my upper neck vertebrae that practically eroded the bone to the point that I was near being paralyzed. If it wasn't for modern medicine (anesthesia, antibiotics, and skillful surgery), I would likely be paralyzed today. I do not know of a natural therapy that would have helped at that point. As I tell my patients in my practice in New York City: "If you get hit by a bus, don't come to my office for herbal therapy, a lifestyle change, and some caring words. Instead, get to the hospital and use all the brilliance modern medical care has to offer." But, for many long-term and chronic illnesses, modern medicine seems to be failing most of us by not addressing the underlying cause, instead using medicines that cover symptoms and do not help the body heal itself.

WHY THIS BOOK?

So why do you need this book? Can't you just take an antidepressant and then feel fine? In the standard medical model, you might think so, as physicians prescribe antidepressants more than any other drugs in the world. In the United States alone, a country with 281 million people, 232.7 million prescriptions were used in 2007, reported IMS Health, mostly to allay symptoms and to provide what was hoped to be a quick fix.

Unfortunately, when it comes to depression, rarely is there a quick fix. The human brain and its moods are very complicated. Some researchers now believe that to say the word *depression* is like saying the word *cancer* in the sense that it may be a group of disorders rather than a single entity. That's why some antidepressants work for some folks (about 30 percent of them) and not for others (about 70 percent of them). Some work well for a while and then stop working. Take the supposed miracle drug Prozac, for instance. Google "Prozac poop out" and you'll find over twenty thousand articles on the problem.

As most people suffering with depression have unfortunately found out, simply popping a pill is not usually a miracle treatment. In fact, despite their incredible popularity and all the marketing hype, antidepressants don't work well for far too many people, and their unpleasant side effects can be stronger than their supposed benefits.

Come with me on a short history of depression for a deeper look at this sorry state of affairs.

YOU WERE LIED TO

Depression was first recognized and treated by Hippocrates, the father of medicine, in the 5th century BC. This disease could render its victims helpless and hopeless, and at its worst, it could even cause death. Hippocrates, in all his brilliance, treated this serious and potentially fatal condition quite successfully with sleep, diet, herbs, and water baths.

As time and science moved on and society became increasingly complex, the medicine of Hippocrates was replaced with newer theories and other ideas—electric shock, lobotomies, talking therapy. However, depression remained an insidious and hidden disease, partially because both sufferers and family members experienced shame and a discouragingly low rate of long-term relief.

Beginning in the 1960s, miraculous drugs were developed to combat this terrible condition. And truly miraculous they appeared to be. These drugs touted a success rate of up to 90 percent for the 25 percent of the population that fell victim to this condition. In the next three decades, such medications vaulted to the top class of all drugs sold, with over $20 billion spent annually.

Despite this rapid pharmaceutical success, most people were not getting better. In 2002, the World Health Organization declared this problem to have, surprisingly, worsened. Then in 2008, the reason for the worsening situation emerged as the medical world was rocked by a study from the *New England Journal of Medicine*. It revealed that the public had been deceived: 31 percent of Food and Drug Administration studies on these had purposely not been published. The courageous authors of this paper explained that even the studies on the effectiveness of antidepressants that were published were erroneously skewed to represent positive results, even though the actual study statistics were negative. Other studies had already shown that these drugs were causing a host of problems including sexual side effects, infertility, increased risk of weight gain and diabetes, blood pressure problems and cardiac deaths, heart defects in unborn children, and even suicide. In 2010, researchers finally decided to look at all the studies in an unbiased approach, and they published in the *Journal of the American Medical Association* that even though millions and millions of people were prescribed these medications, most of the people using them actually gained little or no benefit except in the most severe cases. Despite this definitive research, the medical world continues to treat depression with the same drugs. And to add to the magnitude of the problem, a recent *Journal of Clinical Psychiatry* study of twenty thousand people revealed that more than a quarter of Americans who are taking antidepressants have never been diagnosed with depression or anxiety and therefore could be exposed to side effects from these medications without any proven benefits.

Does this sound too outrageous to be true? Unfortunately, it's completely true. So what is a person suffering with depression or low mood supposed to do?

WHAT THIS BOOK CAN OFFER YOU

In this book, I give you comprehensive yet easy-to-follow solutions that I have seen work for people like you. The best treatments for depression, it turns out, are integrative methods that combine both natural and properly used conventional methods in order to address the source of the depression while providing real and sustainable results.

How Come They're Happy and I'm Not? is designed to build upon what Hippocrates already knew: that natural treatments are safe and effective to deal with depressive illness. But it's not antidrug. I will discuss when pharmaceuticals are appropriate and when it's safe and beneficial to combine natural remedies with conventional care. I will also address beneficial and possible risk interactions. Then I will talk about integrated methods to help those of you on medications safely wean yourselves off and avoid depression relapse.

I will show you why pharmaceuticals, or any single natural remedy for that matter, will likely not cure your mood. Mood disorders are not caused by one factor but instead by many factors that have synergized over the years to create the way you feel now.

In this spirit, I will explain the many possible underlying causes such as inflammation, digestive problems, low nutrient levels, stress, spiritual concerns, and disease, and I will recommend specific lab tests that can further direct your attention to the particular underlying causes of your depression. Then, depending on what we find, I will recommend specifics to bring to your doctor in order to tailor an integrative treatment plan. And of course I will recommend appropriate dietary, exercise, and other therapeutic options for self-healing. You can also check my website if you want to learn more about the research behind the recommendations.

BREAK IT DOWN

Despite being comprehensive, this book is designed to be read by people dealing with depression. Usually that means they have pretty low energy and motivation—so it better be easy. Part I offers easy steps for finding your way to help. I will ask some basic questions to guide you to advice that will be most useful, and I will suggest the top things to do right away to experience relief. Once you are feeling better, you can read the other chapters to receive more comprehensive support.

You will learn that, in the majority of cases, depression is the body's natural response to external stressors and/or internal imbalances and that there are many choices unique to your circumstance to heal the underlying illness. There are reasons for your feelings, and there are real, natural solutions. There's hope.

PART I

The Quick Solution—
Why They Are Happy

1

Owner's Manual to This Book

Most people treat the office manual the way they treat a software manual . . . nobody ever looks at it.

—James Levine

If you're reading this, chances are you don't feel very happy right now. Because of that, I will keep this "owner's manual" chapter short so you get right to the information you need.

Besides not feeling very happy, there's probably another reason you are reading this book: because somewhere inside your body and mind, you genuinely believe there's more in this world for you to do and achieve, but your mood is stopping you from doing it. And you are hoping, after everything you have been through, all the books you have seen, and the advice you've read on the web, watched on TV, and heard from friends or family, that this book might actually be helpful.

There's a reason I wrote this book: because my experience with patients tells me you can use how you are feeling now to eventually move on to be the best you possible. This book is based on my experience with thousands of patients who were in the same position as you.

The last thing you need to do right now is to have to wade through a lot of confusing pages of medical facts and drug bashing, jump through hoops, and read stories of people who are now well. Instead, you probably want simple solutions to feeling better that are easy to do and will work quickly. I know because I've helped thousands of people just like you.

Don't despair; help is on the way.

The truth is, there are many wonderful books out there about depression, all with excellent information. In fact, I list some of them in the resources section of this book because I believe when people are challenged, it's good to gather information from many perspectives as a way to learn from many different angles. These are all well-meaning books, but they are usually afflicted with one of two issues: either they are too long and include too much for readers who do not feel well to wade through, or they are missing important details.

My sincere hope and belief is that this book does not fall into either pitfall. This book is designed for people with depression and low mood to be able to first use easy steps. Then I will offer more extensive discussion, medical facts, and hoops to jump through later on, when you are ready.

One of the major issues I have seen in many of my patients with depressive illness is the inability to start and complete tasks. When you're depressed, the simplest tasks become difficult, due to either lack of motivation or physical symptoms that are just too great to traverse.

Although depression is a complex condition, this book is designed to make help as simple as possible. It offers quick and easy steps that a depressed person or a loved one can take to experience fast relief.

First read the short second chapter, which gives the basics for anyone looking to create a healthier mood. Start implementing as many of these suggestions as possible. If you do not read any other part of this book, just read chapter 2 and try your best to accomplish as many of these steps as possible. These steps will not be all accomplished in a day, I assure you. But that is just fine—the important thing is to get started.

If at all possible, I recommend that you read chapter 2 with a supportive person who can help you organize your schedule and can check in on your progress. Pick someone with whom you feel secure. If you do not have someone like that in your life right now, that is okay too. You can do it on your own just as well.

Which parts of the book should you read after chapter 2? To figure that out, please read through the following and find the description that best fits you:

For males and females age 15 or older: Read chapters 2 through 6 first. Read chapter 7 if you are taking antidepressant medication. Read the "Gender Differences" section of chapter 8.

For seniors: Read chapter 2 first. then the "Seniors" section of chapter 8. If you are on medication, read chapter 7. Finally, you can read all the basics in chapters 3 through 6.

For anyone taking medications: Read chapters 2 and 7 first; then follow with the rest of the book starting with chapter 3.

Please note that there is a lot of information in this book. Don't worry about reading it cover to cover to start; I don't want you to feel overwhelmed. You can start slowly and skip to the sections that seem the most useful for you. You can do it in parts, a little at a time. Take it at your own pace. You can also refer to the site map located at the back of the book. It is a comprehensive list of all recommended therapies with concise information on when to use them. Feel free to refer to this framework as you traverse the book at whatever speed works for you.

Remember, you are doing a great job: the fact that you are reading this means your brain and body want to be united as one happy being living to your greatest potential. The fact that you are reading this means you want to be well, and that is the most important (and often the most difficult) step.

2

The Fast Lowdown of What to Do: The Top Seven Steps to Healing Depression

We also rejoice in our sufferings, because we know that suffering produces perseverance; perseverance, character; and character, hope.

—ROMANS 5:3–4

While this book is filled with over 17 years of research and clinical experience, this chapter avoids the details of all that, by distilling it down to a quick guide to what really works.

You may not be able to do all the steps I suggest here, but try your best to do what you can. Any one of these can help, and the more you do, the better you'll feel. Later in the book, I'll discuss these steps in more detail as well as offer other actions you can take to support your well-being even further.

STEP 1: DETERMINE IF YOU SHOULD BE TAKING MEDICATION

It's not safe to discontinue medication without speaking to your doctor first. If you're taking antidepressant medication, even if you don't feel it's helping, it's best to stay on it for now and let your doctor know that you'll be trying natural medicines. You can share this book with her to help with that discussion if you'd like.

If you believe your medication is helping you, then consider the medication a blessing. Some people get so depressed that they are unable to take the natural steps to help themselves out of the depression. If this was you, and now medication is helping, then that is a good thing. Now you're in a better place to add in the other treatments you'll learn about here. We will work on safely weaning you off the medications later in the book.

If you're having side effects from the medication and you think it is making you feel worse, tell your doctor. He may want to change the dose or switch the medication you're taking. Typical side effects of depression medication include irritability, suicidal thoughts, difficulty falling asleep, excessive hunger, loss of sexual appetite, and weight gain. The younger a person is, the more likely she will experience the side effect of an urge to take her own life. If you're having suicidal feelings, go immediately to your doctor or hospital. They can help you.

If you are not on medication, please take this simple quiz to help you decide if medication is a good idea for you:

1. Does your mood stop you from taking care of yourself (for instance, you do not bathe or eat regularly)?

2. Does your mood stop you from going to work and doing the basic things you need to do to earn a living?

3. If you have children or people who depend on you for their life, does your mood stop you from taking proper care of them?

4. Have you had thoughts of suicide or the idea that you would be better off if you were not around?

If you answered yes to any of these questions, then you should talk with a psychiatrist or physician now. As a naturopathic physician, I do not recommend drugs when other alternatives are available—drugs should be a last resort. But there are occasions when medications may be appropriate to help you in the short term if you are not at a place to help yourself. My recommendation is to look for a licensed naturopathic physician (see the resources section at the end of the book for help finding one) or holistic psychiatrist who can provide medication while starting to work with the natural solutions in this book.

STEP 2: ASK YOUR DOCTOR TO RUN CERTAIN TESTS

It's true that a blood test by itself has never cured anyone. However, the information from particular blood tests can be invaluable to truly understand what is going on in your body and brain. Changes in blood sugar, levels of certain nutrients and hormones, and digestive function can all significantly impact your mood. Having the blood tests I list below can help you make the best choices to help your mood. Make a copy of the blood test list and take it to your doctor as soon as you can.

It's helpful to fast for eight hours before these tests—which means not consuming anything by mouth except water. If you are a female of menstruating age, please tell your doctor where you are in your cycle. If possible, women who are menstruating should have their blood drawn on the first day of flow for best interpretation of estrogen and progesterone values.

This list of recommended blood tests is a valuable tool, especially when you meet with your doctor.

The results of these tests can help us determine the best nutritional supports for your needs. More about how to interpret these blood tests and make decisions focused on your individual needs can be found in chapter 4. Please visit my website for a downloadable detailed blood test list you can bring to your doctor today (*www.drpeterbongiorno.com/happybloodtests*).

RECOMMENDED BLOOD TESTS

Fasting blood sugar and serum insulin
Chemistry panel
Lipid panel

Homocysteine
C-reactive protein
Complete blood count and iron panel
Thyroid Panel
Parathyroid
DHEA and DHEA-S
Testosterone
Estrogen and progesterone (if female)
Celiac panel
Serum carnitine
Serum folic acid and B12
MTHFR Gene Variant
Serum 25 (OH) vitamin D
Serum mercury
ABO Blood Type and Rh

STEP 3: START TAKING THESE SUPPLEMENTS IMMEDIATELY

Vitamins, minerals, and healthy oils are the molecules our bodies use to create reactions that help us make energy, create hormones, and balance immune function, not to mention aiding in a host of other necessary factors for best health. Getting a full range of these is a good start to moving your body and brain in the right direction.

A Potent Multiple Vitamin-Mineral Formula

Neurotransmitters are chemicals that help your body's cells communicate effectively with your brain's nerve cells. When these communicate well, your mood is at its best. Vitamins are molecules that help your body make the neurotransmitters it needs. In particular, B vitamins and magnesium are essential to the process of making neurotransmitters. The better quality vitamins are usually capsules containing powder (as opposed to hard tablets), and high-quality vitamins are usually dosed at four to six capsules a day. Follow the dosage on the bottle and take with food.

Fish Oil

Studies have shown that when people have a daily dose of at least 1,000 mg of eicosapentaenoic acid (EPA), from fish oil, it helps them maintain a positive mood as well as good overall health. The best fish oil available is the triglyceride form (you can find this written on the label). Because fats and oils can carry many environmental toxins, it's important to make sure fish oil is molecularly distilled (it should also say this on the label) and comes from a reputable company. I do not recommend buying fish oil from a large chain store. Always check the expiration date.

Fish oil can be taken as a gel cap or a liquid. Liquid fish oil should be kept in the refrigerator after opening. If you have stomach trouble—and many patients with low mood do—or you find the fish oil makes you burp uncomfortably or gives you reflux, look for an enteric-coated version, which does not cause this discomfort. People taking anticoagulant medications (sometimes referred to as blood thinners) should check with their doctor before taking fish oil. If you're allergic to fish or vegan, you may want to try a vegetable-based essential fatty acid like algae oil, flax oil, or combined omega-3 oils including primrose or sesame. Vegetable oils are typically not as potent, but they're better than not taking any healthy oils.

Vitamin D

Known as the happy vitamin, vitamin D acts like a hormone in the body and has important effects on mood. The list of blood tests I suggested in step 2 includes one for 25(OH) vitamin D level, which is a specific form of vitamin D in the body. It's best to check your D level first if you can and then to decide on the optimal dose of vitamin D. If you cannot check your vitamin D levels anytime soon and want to start feeling better, simply take 4,000 IU a day of the form vitamin D$_3$. If your levels are low, it should help give them a boost. Take vitamin D$_3$ with food for best absorption.

We will talk more about all these supplements as well as other nutrients in chapter 5.

STEP 4: MOVE YOUR BODY

Exercise is a powerful antidepressant. The problem is that when you don't feel good, it's hard to motivate yourself to get out there. For now, do the best you can to exercise for twenty-five minutes every day, and we'll talk more about motivation in chapter 6.

The best form of exercise includes being outdoors with sunlight and trees, which can also boost mood. Jogging, walking, and tai qi are all wonderful. If you have physical limitations, you can try swimming or other gentle movement. A few of my patients who can't walk or move their legs use a tabletop pedal exerciser to move their upper body.

We will discuss exercise further in chapter 3. For now, try your best to do something every day. Anything you can do will be very helpful.

STEP 5: ADD THESE FOODS TO YOUR DIET

Certain foods have powerful mood-enhancing properties. If you are not already eating these "happy foods," try adding them to your daily diet:

- Water: It is necessary to get proper amino acids into the brain. Drink sixty ounces a day, with one big glass first thing in the day.

- Raw nuts and seeds: Eat a total of one cup of these throughout the day. Good choices are almonds, walnuts, sunflower seeds, and pumpkin seeds. Try not to eat roasted nuts.

- Fish: Eat fish three times a week. Wild salmon or rainbow trout are great choices. Canned sardines or anchovies are good if you cannot find fresh fish or do not have the urge to cook it.

- Green vegetables: Eat one every day. A cup of broccoli or spinach is a great choice. If you do not cook, eat two ribs of celery.
- Fruit: Eat one fruit every day.

There are many other healthy foods that are excellent for the brain and your mood. These will be discussed further in chapter 3.

STEP 6: GET THE RIGHT AMOUNT OF SLEEP

Sleep has a profound impact on mood. You should sleep seven to eight hours per night. If you are not sleeping enough, do your best to go to bed earlier in the evening, preferably before midnight. If you are sleeping too much, try your best to create a schedule with a time to go to bed and then set an alarm with gentle, happy music to get you up in the morning. An ideal sleep schedule would be going to bed by ten or eleven p.m. and waking up by six or seven a.m. If you have a hard time falling asleep, try to keep your room dark at night and avoid the TV, computer, or texting at least a half hour before bed.

Sleeping too much or too little can be challenging when you are depressed. More about sleep is in chapter 3.

STEP 7: ADD THESE SUPPLEMENTS IF YOU ARE TAKING MEDICATION

Certain nutritional supplements have been shown in clinical research to be helpful while you are taking antidepressant medications. In many cases, taking these supplements helped people when the medication alone was not effective. The following short list can be easily and safely added to your regimen:

- Folic acid: 15 mg per day. This B-related vitamin has been shown to help people who didn't respond with just medication. The most effective form of folic acid is L-methyl tetrahydrofolate and is superior to the more common folic acid form.
- B_{12}: 1 mg per day (or the bottle might say 1,000 mcg, which is an equal dose). Studies have shown that higher blood levels of

this vitamin help people respond to medication better. Methyl-cobalamin is the best form of B_{12}.

- Zinc: 25 mg per day. Zinc levels are often low in people with depression, and taking zinc has been shown to help raise mood in people who are already using medication.

All the above nutrients can be taken with food.

YOUR SEVEN-STEP CHECKLIST:

1. Check whether you need to take a medication—if yes, visit a physician.
2. Ask your doctor to run blood tests.
3. Take a potent multiple vitamin (full dose), fish oil (1,000 mg of EPA), and vitamin D (2,000 IU).
4. Exercise for twenty-five minutes every day.
5. Foods to add: water (60 ounces daily), raw nuts and seeds (1 cup daily), fish (3 times a week), green vegetable (1 every day), fruit (1 every day).
6. Get to bed by ten or eleven every night.
7. If you take medication, add folic acid (15 mg), B_{12} (1 mg), and zinc (25 mg) every day.

HAVE HOPE

I have seen the preceding seven simple steps help many patients like you feel much better in a matter of weeks. My hope is that these will help you feel better soon, and that you will read the rest of this book to learn more about your particular body and how to keep yourself even happier and healthier in the long term. You deserve to feel good and to enjoy life—and you can!

PART II

Filling in the Details

3

What Happy People
Have in Common

Positivity, yes. Have you had your plus sign today?

—PRINCE

Okay, great. You have already read chapter 2 and have started working on some of the quick suggestions for feeling good. You should congratulate yourself for making a commitment to feeling better. Believe it or not, making that commitment to yourself and acting on it may be the hardest step in the process. Because you have read this far, it's clear you are past that one difficult step. Remember, you do not have to read this book cover to cover. Continue reading as it feels right, and do not worry about skipping chapters and taking only what you need.

To move to a more global scale, it is interesting to look at the happiest people in the world: according to a 2010 Gallup Poll of 140 countries, Denmark, Finland, and the Netherlands were the happiest countries. The poll asked about personal sense of well-being and life satisfaction. While wealth had a role, it seemed that money was clearly not the greatest factor, for countries like New Zealand, with limited money per person, still scored in the top ten. Also, other research from the *British Medical Journal* already showed that even as people tend to make more money, they do not necessarily become any happier.

This Gallup Poll went on to explain that community networks (such as church groups, social organizations, and volunteering communities) as well as family and regular social interaction affected people's happiness. Another important factor was the balance between work and life, specifically avoiding overworking. It reminds me of the adage "Americans live to work, while Europeans work to live." Well, Europe dominated the top of the list, while the United States did not even crack the top ten (it was number twelve). This information tells us we have control over the greatest factors of our own happiness: social interaction and balanced work.

You might ask, "Well, if I weren't depressed, then I could get up and work on social interaction." This is the reason we need to start dealing with your individual physiology too. This book is founded on the idea of trusting in the innate ability of the body to heal itself—the Latin term for this is *vis medicatrix naturae*. Most of my patients with depression come in to my office truly believing that their body cannot heal and that they are stuck in an irreversible pattern. I want you to know that this feeling is just that—a feeling—and it's not true. Happy people eventually understand that feeling is not correct and that their body and mind can feel good again.

Take note of when you get a paper cut—even though the skin is separated, and possibly cut down to the point where blood is released, the body still knows how to fix that—whether you believe it or not. It takes time, and it requires nutrients and blood flow to bring the damaged area what it needs to patch up the wounded vessels and tissue, and eventually heal the skin. Your mood is not much different. With depression, the body is in a difficult pattern. With the right support, your body knows how to fix this.

Are people who do not have depression simply lucky? Maybe . . . but my clinical experience tells me that you can also create a fair bit of your own luck by giving your body the things it needs to heal.

This chapter starts you on that process by recommending and explaining the food, exercise, sleep, and spiritual and emotional ideas that can catalyze your body's ability to rebalance.

DIET

While it sounds simple, the food we eat and the beverages we take in play a major role in our long-term emotional and physical well-being. While some people do not see food as medicine, I would like you to consider diet one of your strongest allies for feeling great in the long term.

Hippocrates said, "Let food be your medicine and medicine be your food." Like many wise adages, this one holds true today, although in the last hundred or so years, we have lost sight of what healthy food is. In fact, in the interest of getting healthier, we have mistakenly turned to harmful foods and eating practices.

So how can food help improve your mood and your brain? Healthy food

- Contains information the body needs to balance by turning on the healthy genes and turning off the unhealthy ones
- Gives the body the nutrients and cofactors it needs to make the right chemicals and neurotransmitters for a happy mood
- Lowers inflammation in the body, improving your mood
- Balances blood sugar, making you less susceptible to mood problems
- Allows the intestines to release toxins that hinder nervous system function

So which foods are truly helpful?

Water

A healthy body and mind require plenty of water. One of my sage naturopathic teachers, Dr. Bill Mitchell, used to say, "When someone has a difficult condition and they aren't drinking enough water, tell them to take an herb in the form of a pill—any gentle herb, and tell them they need to drink it with a big glass of water three times a day—in most cases, their condition will improve quickly." This slightly devious and well-meant suggestion may be right on target for depression.

The human brain is 78 percent water. When we do not have enough water, middle brain areas (called the hypothalamus, limbic, and somatosensory areas) overactivate, creating a stress response and causing low mood.

Low Water → Thirst → Stress Activation → Low Mood

Water is needed for the amino acid tryptophan to be transported to the brain. Tryptophan is converted to serotonin, an important neurotransmitter that allows us to enjoy good mood, remain hopeful and optimistic, keep patient, and help us think things through. Proper serotonin levels also help us avoid sweet and carbohydrate cravings. These cravings are responsible for overeating.

How much water should you be drinking? The general rule is to drink one ounce for every two pounds you weigh every day. So, if you weigh 120 pounds, it's reasonable to drink around sixty ounces (almost two quarts). A person who weights two hundred pounds can drink about ninety to one hundred ounces.

If you do not enjoy the taste of plain water, you can drink herbal teas. Hibiscus tea is naturally sweet and helps balance blood fats. Chamomile tea is calming if you are also feeling anxious. Many of my patients enjoy herbal berry teas and add a little honey. Some of my patients use stevia, which is an herb that has a sweet taste but is actually beneficial for balancing blood sugar. Avoid adding sugar or imitation sweeteners. Drink fluids at room temperature or on the warm side—in Chinese medicine, cold fluids are believed to "put out the belly fire" and shut down digestion. We will learn in chapter 4 that healthy and robust digestion is a key to long-term good mood.

Food as Information

Now that we have discussed the importance of water, let's talk about that solid matter we ingest on a daily basis: food.

Food is the source of protein, carbohydrates, fats, vitamins, and minerals that your body uses to repair, build, detoxify, and energize. Your body knows how to fix problems, but it needs the right stuff to do it. You can think of food as information: the way a computer needs good information in its programming to run properly, your body gets its good information from the food you eat.

It's likely that if you suffer from depressive symptoms, your body is lacking the nutrients and information it needs to keep you healthy. Nutrient deficiencies are found to be very common in depressed patients. For example, it's known that low magnesium in your body can lead to depression by increasing inflammation in the body and the brain. Magnesium deficiency occurs in about 80 percent of people who have depression and is easily remedied by drinking mineral water or eating Swiss chard, molasses, or pumpkin seeds. More about magnesium, one of my all-time-favorite nutrients, is in chapter 5.

Generally, high-quality whole foods, including varied types of vegetables and fruits as well as adequate fiber and protein sources, are crucial to physical and mental health. Stressed-out systems like those of depressed patients require these even more.

One SAD Diet

So are people getting the nutrients they really need? Sadly, the answer is a clear no. Most of us consume the standard American diet, which can be shortened to SAD. Aptly named, this diet fails to provide the high-quality nutrients (such as B vitamins) necessary for metabolic processes, the antioxidant protection (such as vitamins E and C) you need to protect your cells, or the necessary protein and amino acids (like tryptophan) needed to make mood neurotransmitters. In SAD, vegetable intake is low, grains are stripped of valuable nutrition, produce is laden with pesticides, and food comes in plastic containers that release toxins into the food. Highly processed foods are missing nutrients and cannot deliver the same healthy messages to your body that whole foods can. Pesticides and plastics increase the likelihood of diabetes, cardiovascular disease, and inflammation—all of which raise the likelihood of depression (more about toxins and depression in chapter 4).

I Eat Healthy—Am I Getting the Nutrients I Need?

Research shows that even people who try to eat healthy are in trouble. A 2006 study by the American Dietetic Association reviewed approximately seventy diets from a cross section of people ranging from elite athletes who watched their dietary intake carefully to sedentary people who didn't exercise or take care of themselves. Researchers concluded that all diets in the study fell short of the recommended 100 percent recommended daily allowance of micronutrient levels. Furthermore, the more active the person, the greater the tendency toward deficiency. It seems that even when people eat healthy, the foods are fairly devoid of the nutrients they used to have years ago.

The Mediterranean Diet—the Best Diet of All?

I'm often asked: "Dr. Peter, which is the best diet?"

To answer that question, I would like to share a personal story with you:

Despite the fact that medical school should be a place to learn about health, my first year of medical school at the naturopathic program at Bastyr University in Seattle was filled with stress as I did my best with a volume of information that appeared beyond my capacity. The choices I made included spending more hours studying at the expense of exercise and sleep. There was lots of reading and memorizing, and my eating focused on quick foods, usually in the form of carbohydrates to feed a brain that was looking for glucose. While the brain makes up about 2 percent of the mass in our body, it burns through about half the calories the body uses. This is why frenetic students (and stressed-out people in general) love to eat cookies, bagels, and cakes. Ironically, while I was studying health, I was becoming less healthy. By my second year, I had insomnia, anxiety, and regular bouts of heart palpitations and irritability. Although I was not depressed, my mood gradually lowered as the months of insomnia continued.

In the early summer, my Italian immigrant parents booked a trip to Sicily in the early summer. Knowing I was not feeling well, they asked me to join them. My mother said: "You will feel better—you should come." I was feeling so awful, I was sure taking a trip to Sicily and being five thousand miles away from my Seattle home would only make me worse. Luckily, Italian mother guilt got to me, and I agreed to go.

I met my parents in Sicily near my father's coastal hometown after a sixteen-hour trip via New York, Rome, and Palermo. Worried about me, the first thing my mother did—like any loving Italian mother—was make me a meal. This one featured Sicilian olive oil, fresh fish, locally grown vegetables, a small slice of fresh artisan bread, and a little wine. The fish there is so fresh, it's not even kept on ice—it's caught in the waters nearby, wrapped in seaweed, and sold within hours. After I ate, I did what any Sicilian man would do: I took a nap in the sun.

By the next day, I was sleeping like a baby, and my anxiety and physical symptoms had vanished! Now, this is no double-blind placebo controlled study—the kind modern research uses to validate a particular treatment. But when I look back now, I often wonder if all I needed was some good Mediterranean sun and food—the kind of food that kept my ancestors healthy, the kind of food Hippocrates gave to his patients.

Think about it: I had been living through the dark gray Seattle days for over a year and had not seen much sun or been converting vitamin D. Plus my food intake was primarily bready foods for quick energy. That was the first time I'd had sun, healthy oils, fresh fish fatty acids, and vibrant green nutrients in all that time—it was like telling my body, "Don't worry; you are going to be all right."

So, to answer the diet question, if I didn't know a particular individual or her history, I would probably recommend the Mediterranean diet. While no diet is perfect for every individual, there's reason to believe the Mediterranean diet may be the choice for treating mood problems.

Mediterranean Diet Studies

The Mediterranean Sea is the body of water bordering Spain, France, Italy, and the northern coast of Africa. The region touts many beautiful foods and eating rituals associated with a healthy mood.

In 2009, the Spanish government funded a detailed study of the Mediterranean diet. After four and a half years of studying ten thousand people, researchers concluded that those who ate a Mediterranean diet were about half as likely to develop depression. Specifically, the more fruits and nuts a person ate, the less depression was likely. This was also true for beans and healthy oils like olive oil. According to these researchers, aspects of this diet improve blood vessel lining and its function, lower inflammation, and reduce the risk for heart disease. All these effects can decrease the chances of developing depression.

THE MEDITERRANEAN DIET DEFINED

- High ratio of monounsaturated fatty acids to saturated fatty acids*
- Moderate alcohol intake
- High intake of legumes*
- High intake of whole grain cereals and breads
- High intake of fruits and nuts*
- High intake of vegetables
- Low intake of meat and meat products
- Moderate intake of milk and dairy products
- High fish intake

*Denotes foods mostly correlated with low depression risk

According to researchers:

> The membranes of our neurons are composed of fat, so the
> quality of fat that you are eating definitely has an influence
> on the quality of the neuron membranes, and the body's
> synthesis of neurotransmitters is dependent on the vita-
> mins you're eating . . . . We think those with lowest adher-
> ence to the Mediterranean dietary plan have a deficiency
> of essential nutrients . . . . However, the role of the overall
> dietary pattern may be more important than the effect
> of single components. It is plausible that the synergistic
> combination of a sufficient provision of omega-three fatty
> acids together with other natural unsaturated fatty acids
> and antioxidants from olive oil and nuts, flavonoids, and
> other phytochemicals from fruit and other plant foods and
> large amounts of natural folates and other B vitamins in
> the overall Mediterranean dietary pattern may exert a fair
> degree of protection against depression.

Coffee

Mediterranean people also drink a lot of coffee. A 2011 study published in *Archives of Internal Medicine* suggests that the more coffee
women drink, the less likely they are to develop depression. A ten-
year study of fifty thousand nurses found that women who drank
two to three cups a day had a 15 percent lower depression risk. Those
drinking four or more cups a day had a 20 percent decrease. However, tea and decaf coffee showed no difference in the rate of depression. While coffee may be preventative, it's unclear whether it can
help someone who already has depression, and the effect on men is
unknown. Avoid coffee if you have anxiety or insomnia.

Blood Sugar Strategies

Ever know someone who is just in the lousiest mood whenever he is
hungry? Are you one of those people? Hunger and low blood sugar
are primitive signals known to set off a person's stress response.

Humans are animals—and animals are unhappy when their blood sugar is low. It's an evolutionary mechanism designed to make finding food a priority. While this focus helps us avoid starvation, it also triggers anxiety and depression. For those of you who know your mood is affected by hunger, it's very important to eat small meals every two to three hours. Choose foods and snacks that have protein (like almond butter on an apple slice) as opposed to simple carbohydrates (like a cookie). The simple carbs spike your sugar, which sets off a reaction to surge insulin, which drops your blood sugar even lower than when it started, creating the negative pattern.

This list of ideas for good blood sugar control is a useful reference. I encourage you to copy it and keep it handy.

IDEAS FOR GOOD BLOOD SUGAR CONTROL

- If you tend to have low blood sugar, eat small meals or snacks every two to three hours.
- Meals should include protein: fish, grass-fed meat, eggs, or protein powder in a shake, and some fats: avocado, nut oil, fish oil, olive oil, or coconut.
- Snacks ideas: apple or celery with almond butter, raw nut and seed mix with dark chocolate chips and organic raisins, carrots and hummus.
- Avoid simple carbs like cake, cookies, and bread.

Other Foods Good for the Body and Mind with Depression

While generally eating healthily is good for the brain, specific foods can help a person with poor mood feel better more quickly. The following list includes some of my favorites mood-improving foods as well as those that are best researched. Please start bringing these into your life for your best mood.

Crunchy Vegetables

Do you ever get moody and go to grab a bag of chips? There is a reason why we go for that: crunching noises make us feel better. Research suggests that the crunching sounds reach the brain, allowing pleasure centers to release endorphins. This is probably another evolutionary way to help ensure we eat.

Although chips are not the healthiest option, because crunchy food calms, you can still use this mechanism to your advantage. Carrots, peppers, celery, and other crunchy vegetables have been shown to reduce stress in the same way. Also, there are a number of healthier baked snacks, like flax meal crackers and high bran fiber crackers, that can also fill in for the job. Raw nuts are great too. Roasted nuts may be tasty, but they are not as healthy for the brain and body due to the overcooked oils they absorb. It should also be noted that when people eat too many calories from junky, crunchy foods—their mood darkens.

IDEAS FOR HEALTHY CRUNCH FOODS

- Baby carrots
- Raw nuts: almonds, walnuts, cashews
- Raw seeds: pumpkin seeds, sunflower seeds
- Flax crackers
- Bran or whole fiber crackers
- Crunchy vegetables: peas, carrots, peppers

Super Foods for Low Mood and Depression

Pomegranate

One 2004 study worked with female mice with both depression and low bone density. Mice that drank pomegranate extract had significantly improved mood and normalized bone density. The pomegranate is known to have gentle plant versions of estrogen, called phytoestrogens, which may account for the improved behavior and increase in bone strength. The pomegranate may be a great food for postmenopausal women who experience both depression and have bone density concerns.

Raw Nuts

Eaten by health-conscious people for millennia, raw nuts are chock full of healthy fatty acids, protein, and minerals. Nuts are known for their ability to lower body inflammation. One study found that people who eat nuts regularly have lower blood levels of C-reactive protein (CRP), a marker of inflammation that is strongly correlated with cardiovascular disease. CRP is an even better predictor of heart problems than cholesterol is. Additionally, nuts drastically decrease interleukin-6 (IL-6, an inflammation-causing molecule) and vascular adhesion factors (which cause blood vessel stickiness and clots). CRP and IL-6 are typically quite high in people who are depressed too. The benefit in nuts is probably due to the high levels of fatty acids and magnesium. Healthy raw nuts include almonds, Brazil nuts, chestnuts, and cashews.

Protein

Our world is abundant with food—so much so that 60 percent of people are obese. Yet, I cannot count how many patients have come into my office deficient in protein. Many of us simply do not eat enough protein—although we eat tons of carbs. And when we do eat protein, it comes from antibiotic- and hormone-filled, grain-fed, sedentary animals whose meat is high in saturated fat.

Protein is made of amino acids, and amino acids are the building blocks of your neurotransmitters. In excessive quantity, however, protein can suppress central nervous system serotonin levels and be problematic for anyone with kidney disease or low kidney function.

So finding the right level of protein intake is crucial. Basically, a healthy adult needs a minimum of 0.8 g of protein for every 2.2 pounds of body weight. For example: say you weigh 120 pounds. Divide 120 pounds by 2.2, to get 54.5. Now multiply that number by 0.8, giving the answer of 43.6 g of protein. If you are an avid exerciser, you need more protein and can multiply by 1 g instead of 0.8. Elite athletes (Olympians or professional athletes) should multiply by 1.2 g.

How much protein do you really need?

$$\frac{\text{weight (pounds)} \times 0.8 \text{ g}}{2.2 \text{ (pounds)}} = \underline{\hspace{2cm}} \text{ g of protein you need per day}$$

The best protein sources include fish, grass-fed beef, free-range chicken, beans and legumes, and some soy (like fermented natto and tempeh).

Why Is Grass-Fed Meat So Important? Isn't Natural and Antibiotic-Free Enough?

It's universally accepted that wild fish like salmon, which eat the algae and plankton at the bottom of the sea, are a healthier source of protein than even their coastline fish farm–raised counterparts. Over their life span of eating sea greens, these fish accumulate a wonderful concentration of essential fatty acids in their muscles, contributing to their healthfulness.

What many people do not know, however, is that cows that eat grass also accumulate the same essential fatty acids that wild fish do. However, when range animals are fed grains and corn, they do not collect the same healthy fats in their muscle tissue, and instead collect more saturated, unhealthy fats. Meat that is labeled "natural" or "antibiotic free" simply means that the animals were not treated with nasty hormones or antibiotics to help them grow faster (by the way, 70 percent of antibiotics used in the world are used specifically to make livestock grow faster). Even meat that is labeled "organic" typically comes from animals that were fed grains—not grass. At the health food store, look for "grass fed," not just "natural," "organic," or "antibiotic free" for your meats—your brain and heart will thank you.

TWO OF MY FAVORITE PROTEIN SHAKE RECIPES

Dr. Peter's Recipe

7 ounces water or rice milk
20 grams protein powder
1 teaspoon cinnamon
½ cup frozen organic blueberries or lingonberries
½ banana (frozen is great)

Dr. Pina's Piña Colada

20 grams protein powder
3 ounces low-fat coconut milk
3 ounces pineapple juice
½ cup frozen pineapple chunks or ice

A Good, Fishy, and Fatty Story

One study researching thirteen countries revealed that nations with a high intake of fish have very low rates of depression. There are two main types of healthy omega-3 fatty acids in fish: eicosapentaenoic acid (EPA) and docosahexaenoic acid (DHA), which are especially high in wild salmon, striped bass, mackerel, rainbow trout, halibut, and sardines. While lower DHA content in breast milk and lower seafood consumption are both associated with higher rates of postpartum depression, geographic areas where consumption of DHA is high are associated with decreased rates of depression. Individuals with major depression have marked depletions in omega-3 fatty acids (especially DHA) in blood cell fats compared with people who do not have depression.

The standard American diet (SAD) we discussed earlier tends to be low in healthy omega-3 fish oils and high in omega-6 fats, which are found in saturated fats and red meats. It's well established that diets with high omega-6 to omega-3 ratios increase risk of heart disease and contribute to low mood. Researchers in one Swedish study found that that depressive symptoms and markers of inflammation in senior patients increased with higher omega-6 to omega-3 fatty acid ratios. They concluded that such diets increase not only the risk of cardiovascular disease but also depression.

Because your brain and nervous system are made of fats and water, the fat you eat is very important for your mood. Healthy oils such as cold-pressed extra virgin olive oil (which are called omega-9 fats or oleic acids) and flax oils (omega-3 fats) are highly recommended to put on foods (although flax oil should never be heated). Organic, natural foods and wild fish are a preferred source due to the lower levels of pesticides and neurotoxins that may play a role in some depressive illnesses (see chapter 4 for more about toxins). Hydrogenated oil, fried foods, and non-grass-fed animal-based saturated fats, all of which promote inflammation, are not mood-friendly.

Eating on the Run?

The Horace Fletcher quote "Nature castigates those who do not masticate" is the perfect reminder for how detrimental eating on the run can be. For your best digestion and mood, it's important to do your best to eat in a quiet environment and to chew your food well. Given that most of us skip meals or eat in the car (eating in the car, by the way, accounts for an astounding 80 percent of car accidents), this healthy act alone can be quite an impressive accomplishment. In the past, Americans typically chewed a mouthful of food as many as twenty-five times before swallowing. Currently, the average American chews only ten times before swallowing.

When the food is not broken down well, the immune system in the digestive tract sees larger-than-normal substances that are not ready to be absorbed. This triggers the immune system to create inflammation, making factors called cytokines. Cytokines are basically cells that like turning up the flame—they create inflammation and can even cause fever. When this cytokine cascade is turned on, the blood supply that pumps through the intestines carries cytokines that tell the liver to get inflamed too. In the liver, the cells that do this are called Kupffer cells. The liver releases these to the general circulation, and some reach the brain. In the brain, the signal is received by glial cells, which are specialized brain immune cells that make the brain inflamed and unhappy. Brain inflammation is a major contributor to depression.

Poor Digestion → Gut Inflammation → Liver
Inflammation → Brain Inflammation→ Depression

We talk more about gut inflammation in the digestion section in chapter 4. In the meantime, remember that as part of any healthy eating program, you want to first create a moment to take a deep breath and then eat your food in a relaxed environment. Now try to chew approximately twenty-five times per bite, until the texture of the food is unrecognizable. Proper chewing allows for significantly better digestion, which encourages better nutrient absorption and lower inflammatory reactions in your digestive tract.

Desire to Overeat and Food Addiction

Typically, the foods we find most tasteful are those with generous amounts of fat, sugar, or salt. I notice my own three-year-old daughter, Sophia, gravitates toward fries, cookies, and chips despite the fact that both her parents are naturopathic doctors. Why is that? It's because she is wired to like them.

These fats, sugars, and salty food components stimulate the brain to secrete dopamine, the neurotransmitter of pleasure, as an evolutionary survival mechanism that our ancestors needed to keep weight on during lean times. In the short term, this dopamine boost makes us feel pretty happy—the same way cocaine can give a person a temporary high. But, like cocaine, long-term consumption of these foods is a health disaster. Because we have plenty of food available, this evolutionary mechanism to protect us from starvation is now increasing rates of obesity, cardiovascular disease, depression, diabetes, cancer, and many other common conditions fueled by the foods of our modern age.

As you continue to eat these tasty fatty, sugary, and salty foods, a learned behavior response ensues—even the mere suggestion of the desired food (such as a clever billboard ad or a slick TV commercial) spurs a desire to eat them. Once the food is consumed, the brain releases opioids, which bring emotional relief. In other words: you are addicted. Together, dopamine and opioids create a pathway that activates every time you are reminded about the particular food. This happens regardless of whether you are hungry or not.

Most of us are vulnerable to conditioned overeating. There's a lucky 15 percent of the population that do not have the mechanism of overeating built in to their system, so they are less affected. In primitive times, these people probably would have starved, but now they have the advantage that they can control their response to food.

Sugar and High-Fructose Corn Syrup

Sugar and high-fructose corn syrup (HFCS) are powerful contributors to the food addiction phenomenon—so much so that HFCS in soda is the number one source of calories in the United States! These sugars have a direct detrimental impact on your brain function and an indirect effect on your body through its ability to make you fat. So both thin and thicker persons alike need to stay away from these sweet temptations.

Foods with a lower glycemic load (less sugar per weighted amount of food) should be central to the diet. Vegetables, fruits, and beans; lean organic, grass-fed meats and cold-water fishes; and whole grains are at the top of the list.

EXERCISE

With the "progress" of modern medicine and society over the past hundred years, lifestyle changes that alleviate depression have all but gone by the wayside. The ability to patent and sell medication has trumped all other forms of medical intervention. About 2,500 years ago, Hippocrates recommended regular exercise as treatment for depression. Since then, many common-sense and learned people, both ancient and modern, have used exercise as a means of preventing disease and promoting health and well-being.

Exercise is possibly the strongest single antidepressant we have. Known to elevate mood by reducing anxiety, depression, and negative mood and increasing self-esteem, exercise also improves a number of biological risk factors for depression. It balances blood sugar, raises good cholesterol (which you will learn more about in chapter 4), and improves heart and blood vessel health.

Exercise and Mood

So how does exercise accomplish all these great feats? Modern research shows that when we exercise, our bodies produce helpful molecules which can fix a broken brain. One such molecule is brain-derived neurotrophic factor (BDNF). BDNF is a key player in stimulating the growth of new neurons and pathways that the nerves use to communicate and create better mood.

The hippocampus is an area of the brain that is a key for memory, mood, spatial relationships, and much more. The hippocampus has also been shown to shrink in people who are stressed out much of the time. Exercise, however, can reverse this shrinkage. Collaborative studies between the Salk Institute in California and German universities in the early 2000s found that animals that voluntarily ran wheels showed increased cell building and growing in the hippocampus.

This has been shown not only in animals—this almost magical effect has also been shown in human beings. One 2008 Dutch study of almost six thousand twins found that the more that people exercised, the happier they were. The first-ever proven neurogenesis (nervous tissue generation) within a living human brain was accomplished by exercise. The study, published in 2003, followed eleven people of below-average fitness as they trained four times a week for twelve weeks using the exercise regimen given below. The results showed that exercise targets an area of the hippocampus called the dentate gyrus, which is very important for mood and memory as you age. Some research has shown that when antidepressant medications work, they're likely building up the hippocampus—something that exercise effectively does without drugs.

BEGINNER'S GUIDE TO GROWING YOUR BRAIN'S HIPPOCAMPUS

Four times a week, do the following:

- 1–5 minutes of low-intensity warm-up on a treadmill or stationary bicycle
- 2–5 minutes of stretching
- 3–40 minutes of aerobic activity on a stationary bike, treadmill, stair climber, or elliptical trainer
- 4–10 minutes of cool down and stretching

Is Exercise Better than Drugs?

To compare the benefits of exercise versus medication, researchers assigned 156 adults with major depression aerobic exercise or Zoloft, or a combination of both. After four months, patients in all three groups exhibited improvement, but after ten months, the exercise group had significantly lower relapse rates than the medication group. Additionally, patients who exercised on their own during the follow-up period were less likely to experience depression again. A second study of 156 patients at least fifty years old were prescribed exercise or antidepressants. Initially, the antidepressant group displayed a quicker improvement. But after sixteen weeks, exercise was equally effective as drugs in reducing depression.

What to Do to Get Your Body Going

Level 1:

If you have not exercised before, start with gentle walking outdoors for thirty minutes every day—and you can add more if you like. Walking outside in the morning sun is especially beneficial, for you absorb sunlight, training your biorhythms to help you have more energy during the day and better sleep at night. Exercising outdoors also supports vitamin D levels.

Level 2:

If you have exercised before and would like a stronger plan, you can start the "Beginner's Guide to Growing Your Brain's Hippocampus" regimen (see page 32).

Level 3:

If you are already using the Beginner's Guide and would like more, start a resistance program using free weights and resistance machines two days a week. One day you can exercise your chest, back, biceps, thighs, and abdominals. The second day, you can work out your shoulders, triceps, hamstrings, calves, and again, abdominals. If it's at all possible, I highly recommend working with a trainer for at least a few sessions to teach you proper techniques and the best exercises for your body. You can work out following the Beginner's Guide four days a week, your resistance workout two days a week, and take a day off to relax.

* * *

You may be thinking, I am stuck. What kind of exercise can I do? Even if you have physical ailments that do not allow you to walk outside, there are still ways you can exercise. One sixty-year-old patient, "Marge," came into my office on two diabetes medications, and her blood sugar level was still around 300 (normal range is between 70 and 100). She was experiencing depression, high blood pressure, and diabetes. Supported and balanced by her husband, she walked, inch by inch, into my office.

She had come because her quality of life was reduced to nothing—she was too dizzy to walk more than a few steps. It stopped her from visiting friends and family, and doing anything that made life enjoyable. We decreased Marge's carb intake and increased her water intake. Of course, I recommended exercise and gave her some naturopathic herbs and nutrients for the diabetes issues. Knowing her severe physical limitation for exercise, I recommended she purchase a tabletop arm/leg cycle and exercise her arms for ten minutes twice a day. Over the course of a few months, we included some leg movement with that. That transitioned into walking outside a little bit and then to walking outside more and doing some indoor light resistance work.

Today, Marge is on a low dose of one diabetes medication, has normal blood sugar, and can take full walks outside, visit her friends, and even can go out and "cheat" on occasion when enjoying a nice restaurant with her husband. If someone is in a wheelchair, there are even versions of these cycles that a wheelchair can pull up to. No matter the situation, if there's a body part that can move, there's a way to start exercising and feeling better.

Please note that if you are ready to start exercising but have not really exercised before, it's always a good idea to check with your physician. More than likely, there's not a reason you cannot exercise, but you should start at a level that is safe for you. In my experience, patients who have depression are not held back by a physical issue but rather by a psychological one—motivation. We will talk more about that in chapter 6.

SLEEP

Regular, quality sleep is of paramount importance to your good health. Although some patients with depression sleep too much, the vast majority I have worked with do not sleep enough. Sleep problems are considered a symptom of an underlying depression, and in many cases, sleep problems come before the onset or recurrence of depression. In fact, a survey of office-based physicians revealed that about 30 percent of patients diagnosed with insomnia were also diagnosed with depression. Interrupted or deficient sleep negatively affects your body's biorhythms (also known as circadian rhythm). Imbalanced biorhythms can cause suboptimal immune function and can release extra stress hormones like cortisol.

Why Am I Not Sleeping Well?

About 20 percent of patients with depression suffer from sleep apnea, a disturbed sleep condition characterized by decreases (hypopneas) or pauses (apneas) when breathing. With this condition, affected patients have problems with daytime fatigue, traffic accidents, and blood pressure problems. An obstructive apnea is defined as at least ten seconds interruption of airflow and is associated with a decrease in the oxygen level in your blood, where the primitive part of your brain that monitors oxygen level makes you temporarily wake up, looking for air. Sometimes I ask my patient to ask a partner, "Do I snore, or start and stop breathing when I sleep?" If the answer is yes, I may refer these patients to a pulmonologist (lung doctor) or sleep specialist to explore the issue further.

Naturopathic treatment for sleep apnea may include weight loss, support for the respiratory system, or food sensitivity/allergy work (see chapter 4). Helpful conventional medical treatments include using a continuous positive airway pressure (CPAP) machine at night if the naturopathic treatments are not enough. Some studies have seen clear improvement in depression symptoms using the CPAP machines alone, while others didn't observe improvement. In my experience, although this machine may take getting used to, when patients use it consistently and move past the initial discomfort of the apparatus, they tend to experience improved energy and mood. These benefits far outweigh the initial discomfort felt when first going to sleep with the machine.

Are You a Night Owl?

Bright light exposure can cause a condition called delayed sleep phase syndrome (DSPS), a common but little-reported cause of severe insomnia and depression. A hormone called melatonin is normally released when our eyes sense darkness. This master hormone helps us prepare for sleep and is also a powerful antioxidant known to help the body detoxify, especially when it comes to cancer.

Melatonin's properly timed release plays a key role in keeping optimal mood. Otherwise, people can experience circadian rhythm problems, including symptoms like sleep-onset insomnia (can't fall asleep at night) and waking up too early in the morning. Generally people with DSPS feel more alert at night than in the morning—they are the self-proclaimed night owls. Does this sound like you? Many suffer from the inability to wake up early enough to start their day—these people want to keep sleeping, and once they are up, they experience immeasurable fatigue during the day. The prevalence of depression and personality disorders in DSPS sufferers is very high.

We will talk about how to readjust this cycle later in this chapter.

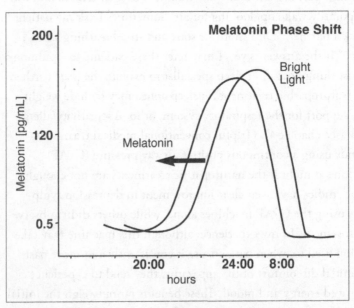

Figure 1: Bright Light Makes Melatonin Get Released Too Late

Your Eight-Step Plan to a Good Night's Sleep

In my practice, focusing on sleep quality is key for many issues: low immunity, muscle repair, mood problems, digestion . . . the list goes on and on. Try these steps if you need a good night's sleep:

Step 1: Find Out if You Have Sleep Apnea

Ask your partner if you snore. Better yet, set up a video camera to record yourself sleeping and see for yourself. Check for signs of heavy snoring and long pauses in breathing. The gold standard way to diagnose this properly is to work with a sleep clinic that studies you while you sleep. If sleep apnea is an issue, work with a naturopathic doctor to help lower inflammation in your nasal passages, which is usually caused by food allergies, and lose weight if you are heavy. If these do not work, or if the condition is severe, you may want to see a pulmonologist or sleep specialist for information about a CPAP machine or even consider surgery to reduce upper respiratory tract extra tissue. However, I recommend trying more natural treatments before resorting to surgery.

Step 2: Be in Bed Before Midnight (and Preferably by Ten P.M.)

There's an old Chinese proverb that says, "One hour before midnight is worth two hours after midnight." This proverb predates what we now understand about the timing of melatonin release. Research shows that melatonin peaks at about ten p.m. and rapidly decreases afterward. Going to bed earlier than midnight takes advantage of that maximum release. Also, the later you go to bed, the more you release stress hormones. You see, animals that stay up past dark are usually either running for their lives or starving—so when you stay up late, you are telling your primitive brain there's a big problem, and it sends out the signal to be stressed. If you are used to going to bed at one a.m. or later, you may need to start by backing up that bedtime by a half hour each week so your body rhythms have a chance to adjust. I recommend taking a melatonin supplement a half hour before the desired bedtime to help you reset your rhythm.

Step 3: Dim All the Lights

Avoid bright lights at least thirty minutes before bed. This includes computers, cell phones, tablets, and televisions. Bright lights suppress the release of melatonin and trick your body into thinking it's still daytime, which triggers a stress response.

Step 4: Create an Evening Ritual

Once you dim the lights, make a calming tea such as chamomile or lavender. It's best to make a small concentrated cup and sip it so you do not fill your bladder too much and have to get up during the night. Over time, you will find comfort in a regular, healthy ritual guiding your body to be calm and relaxed for a successfully sleepy bedtime.

Step 5: Keep Your Bedroom Dark

Hormones like melatonin and human growth hormone are important for repair and detoxification. These are suppressed when the bedroom is too bright. The rule of thumb is: if you can see your hand one foot in front of your face, then the room is too bright. Use electric tape to cover any light sources, and try occlusive blinds that are cracked just at the top to allow morning light in.

Step 6: Check Your Blood Sugar

Some people experience drops in blood sugar before bed and have a hard time entering a deeper sleep due to hunger, which signals your animal body to stay awake to look for food. If this might be you, try eating a protein-and-carbohydrate snack a few minutes before bed. Try a small piece of turkey and a slice of apple, or if you are a vegetarian, try an apple slice with a tablespoon of nut butter.

Step 7: Journal Before Bed

From an emotional standpoint, humans are not created for the hectic modern lives we lead. Oftentimes, our first quiet time of the day is when our head hits the pillow. If there are issues that our brain wants to work out, it may use this quiet time to say, "Okay, I got you here—just the two of us, and there's nothing to distract us, so let's go over a few things . . . ." That is when you start to mentally process your job, kids, in-laws, finances, old relationships, lack of relationships, new dent in the car, world peace, schedule for tomorrow, and so on.

Many of my patients find it helpful to stop for a minute right before bed and journal a bullet point to-do list for the next day. Some also jot down recurrent worries, so we can address them and come up with solutions. You may not be able to fix all the issues at that moment, but if you can convince your brain that you are earnestly working on them, it may allow you to relax for a good night's sleep.

Step 8: If Needed, Use Natural Remedies to Help with Sleep

Try the above steps for two weeks to see if they help your sleep quality. If these are not quite doing the trick, try taking melatonin and herb passion flower (*Passiflora incarnata*) supplements, my favorites from the natural armamentarium. Passion flower tincture or capsules are wonderful for people who are constantly overthinking. Valerian is also a well-studied choice that can help create a better night. If you tend to wake frequently, try taking time-released melatonin (1 to 6 mg), L-tryptophan (1,000 mg), and 5-HTP (100 mg) before bed to help you remain asleep. Motherwort at 20 to 60 drops of a 1:1 tincture in a little water before bed is another herbal choice for people who have trouble staying asleep, but it shouldn't be used by people who have low thyroid function.

SUNLIGHT

We talked about the importance of darkness in the last section, so now let's talk about the importance of light. In medical school, my nutrients teacher Alan Gaby, MD, reminded us of John Denver's famous lyrics: "Sunshine on my shoulder makes me happy." Apparently Denver knew more about sunshine and the role of vitamin D in mood than most doctors do. Sunlight and its dose of vitamin D are a powerful natural curative when it comes to mood. It not only improves mood but may even protect against prostate, breast, and colorectal cancers. Sunlight sends signals through our eyes to the hypothalamus, the brain's communication hub for our body clock, nervous system, immune system, and hormonal system. The hypothalamus modulates melatonin secretion, which affects our sleep and wake cycles. Proper amounts of both light and darkness help balance our circadian rhythm for a healthy body and mood.

CLINICAL CASE: STEVE ON SEROQUEL

A colleague sent his brother, Steve, to my office. Steve was a well-dressed forty-seven-year-old who came to my office explaining how he'd had depression since he was thirty-five. His depression started at the time he was getting divorced following five difficult years of marriage. At the time, his doctor placed him on Wellbutrin, which seemed to alleviate the deeper depression at the time, but it did not fix Steve's generally low mood. His most recent acute bout of depression surfaced about four months before our visit with the loss of his mother just one month after he'd been laid off from his job. His psychopharmacologist added Cymbalta to his eleven-year-old prescription of Wellbutrin.

Steve came in due to terrible insomnia—he had been trying to schedule job interviews, but the insomnia was so severe, he felt as if he could not function at an interview. His psychopharmacologist wanted to add Seroquel, a very strong antipsychotic drug used for bipolar and schizophrenia that generally blocks brain communication and carries a laundry list of short- and long-term side effects, but Steve wanted to try other options.

I started by giving Steve acupuncture weekly, and we settled on dosages of 3 mg of time-released melatonin plus 1,000 mg of tryptophan forty minutes before bed instead of the Seroquel. After a week, these worked, but not consistently enough for Steve to feel he could count on them, and his own body, to sleep well enough for an interview the next day. We then added 500 mg of valerian root extract, which allowed Steve to sleep a full night every night. This allowed his depression to lift significantly, and he restarted his interviewing process.

Consistent with the increase in depression over the past century is the decrease is human exposure to sunlight. Modern life is replete with sunlight blockers: buildings, pollution, vehicle travel, clothing, and medical advice to fear the sun. While shunning the sun can prevent one kind of cancer (skin), it's at the cost of allowing fifty-five other cancers to flourish. And patients with the lowest blood levels of vitamin D are two times more likely to die from any cause, according to a 2008 article in the *Archives of Internal Medicine*.

Regardless of our modern sun-phobic rationale, sunlight exposure is likely needed in various parts of our body, not just our eyes, for healthy circadian function. Photoreceptors are molecules in our body that sense light and send signals to the brain. They are found in the eyes as well as behind the knee. In one study, scientists exposed patients to bright light only behind the knee and found that body rhythm changes resulted. The body may be able to regulate mood with more full-body exposure to light.

Let There Be Light

Serotonin is a neurotransmitter involved with positive feelings like calmness, hope, optimism, and love. Serotonin levels are known to increase with bright light and to be lowest in the winter. Studies have also shown that brain molecules called serotonin transporters, which bind up serotonin and make it inactive, are more plentiful during dark periods.

As discussed, depression has been associated with delayed releases of melatonin in the evening, which can happen when we are exposed to bright light late at night or when we go to bed too late. Research subjects known as morning types typically present with a healthier schedule of earlier sleep onset at night and earlier waking. People who wake up earlier are more likely to have more morning bright light exposure, increasing serotonin levels and decreasing morning melatonin secretion duration, leading to a less depressed mood.

I went to medical school in Seattle, a city that boasts averages of 201 cloudy days, 93 partly cloudy days, and 71 sunny days per year. In my clinic, we saw a ton of depression and low vitamin D. (That's probably why so many people in Seattle love coffee.) I learned early on in my training that for some of my patients with depressed mood, morning sunlight exposure was crucial—especially for treating seasonal affective disorder (SAD), a condition marked by low mood as the days get shorter.

Maybe the Best Mood Study Yet

Light therapy works by decreasing morning melatonin secretion, which sets up the body to release it more robustly in the evening. In a fantastic eight-week study of 112 women ages nineteen to seventy-eight with mild to moderate depression, University of Washington researchers had these women do two things: take a twenty-minute brisk walk outside during daylight hours five days a week and take a multivitamin supplement that included 50 mg each of vitamins B_1, B_2, and B_6; 400 mcg of folic acid; 400 IU of vitamin D; and 200 mcg of selenium. A control group received a placebo and didn't exercise. The group that exercised and took the real vitamins enjoyed decreased depression and improved overall mood, reduced depression symptoms, and increased self-esteem and general well-being. In this study, the combination of morning light, exercise, and vitamins helped 85 percent of the group's mood, a much better effect than we see with medication.

I love this study, for it's one of the very few that uses more than one natural remedy to support the body's own healing process. This is how naturopathic medicine works. Currently, research is conducted mostly on drugs. When natural remedies are researched, they are often studied in isolation—meaning only one treatment is used at a time for patients who have depression. This creates a much slimmer chance of working than if a few different treatments are used at the same time to support the body. Hopefully future research will study combinations of treatments as this one did.

Why Sunlight Is So Helpful

Besides sunlight's ability to suppress daytime melatonin, which contributes to a healthy circadian rhythm, sunlight's other likely contributor to healthy mood is vitamin D. The components of sunlight are visible light, ultraviolet radiation, and infrared radiation. The two ultraviolet wavelengths are ultraviolet A and ultraviolet B, which converts to vitamin D.

One study investigated the importance of ultraviolet light's exposure on skin to mood. In this test, frequent tanners used two different tanning beds over a period of six weeks. The beds were identical except that in one, the ultraviolet light was filtered out. Even though study participants could not tell which bed had the ultraviolet light, they reported that they were more relaxed and less tense after exposure to the bed with ultraviolet light. When allowed to choose which bed to use, eleven of twelve participants chose the one with ultraviolet light. Scientists think ultraviolet light helps the skin transform the cutaneous chemical 7-dehydrocholesterol into vitamin D_3. We will talk a bit more about vitamin D in chapter 5.

Sunlight's infrared wavelengths may also help. A 2007 animal study showed an increase in the amount of time before an animal will show signs of depression under continuous stress when the animals are exposed to infrared irradiation for four weeks. This suggests that a continuous application of infrared irradiation has an antidepressant effect. In my office, I often use an infrared device called a TDP lamp while giving patients acupuncture to help with their mood. Patients tell me the lamp makes them feel secure and nourished as well as warm during their acupuncture session.

How to Put Yourself in the Best Light

The first step to healthy sunlight exposure is to get out there into nature, whether it's for a walk in a park or an early morning jog. If weather permits, wear less clothing to allow the sunlight to reach your skin. Some reports claim that ten to twenty minutes of full sun exposure per day—during non-peak sun—provide enough healthy sun effects without causing the damage. To see if your skin is getting too much sun, look at your skin through a good set of sunglasses—if you start to see some redness, it's time to cover up. One journal article reports that twelve minutes of noontime, cloudless sun exposure on 50 percent of the skin is equivalent to oral intake of 3,000 IU of vitamin D_3. Keep in mind that if you are at high risk for skin cancer, you may need to be more cautious. A vitamin D supplement and light box phototherapy may be good alternative solutions.

A second step, if needed, would be phototherapy, or light box therapy. This can be used to treat depressive illness, and it is particularly useful for obvious cases of fall and winter seasonal affective disorder, although I have seen light therapy help general depression and sleep issues. Treatment, typically prescribed for mild to moderate depression, consists of exposure to full-spectrum white light (at a power of 10,000 lux) for at least thirty minutes every morning. There is no known risk of light therapy.

STRESS

Whether it's related to family, work, relationships, or money, stress is a major factor in depression. This is recognized in both written literature and research. In animal studies, short-term stress causes us to respond to our world, which is healthy. But chronic stress (the kind we humans seem to sustain) decreases an animal's ability and encourages withdrawal-type behaviors associated with depression.

As a researcher at the National Institute of Mental Health, I studied the effect of stress on animals. What I learned is that if you want to make an animal depressed, all you need to do is stress it out every day for a few weeks. You may be saying, "I know what that feels like." Well, if your life is a chronic stress, you are participating in a depression experiment of your own.

You may be interested to know that the standard animal model of depression consists of subjecting an animal to a random schedule of severe, uncontrollable stress until the animal withdraws into a shell of "learned helplessness." Oftentimes, I explain this when I lecture to medical students, and invariably, some overworked, harried, half-awake medical student or resident (who sat in my talk not so much because of my charisma, but more likely due to the free lunch or dinner) will raise her hand and say, "Hey, that sounds like my life."

Chronic stress in animals creates similar inflammatory profiles and behavior patterns as those seen in humans with depression. (We will talk a lot more about inflammation in the next chapter.) Stressed animals stop drinking sweet water that they formerly enjoyed—this behavior change is likened to anhedonia in humans—an inability to experience pleasure from normally pleasurable life events. Anhedonia can be a core symptom of depression. The hypothesis correlating the symptoms in animals with those in humans is that chronic mild stress (CMS) induces a change in brain reward function that resembles the symptoms of major depression—namely, a decrease in responsiveness to rewarding stimuli.

Another classic stress model with rats amounts to a mild torture that is minor enough not to hurt the animal overtly but over time causes its mood to plummet. In detail, researchers house rats individually and subject them to a light electric shock to the foot for ten seconds per minute for thirty minutes, and then have the animal fast for forty-eight hours. Then researchers have the rats swim in ice water for five minutes, followed by deprivation of water for twenty-four hours, after which they are subjected to a warm room for five minutes, followed by tottering (walking on unstable ground) for fifteen minutes. Finally, researchers squeeze the rats' tails for one minute. This stress is repeated two to three times in the course of twenty-one days. This mild torture creates the same functional effect in the rats' brain and behavior as we see in human depression. When you think about your own depression, you may want to outline the tortuous route you take, not for self-pity, but instead to understand how to break this cycle. We are going talk about different ways to handle stress in chapter 6.

YOUR BRAIN ON TELEVISION

Television's role in influencing the mental and physical state of our society has been profound. In the short term, TV seems to have a relaxing effect. A 2004 article in *Neuroimage* details studies using functional MRI during TV viewing that have determined that humorous television programming can activate regions of the brain called the insular cortex and amygdala, areas needed for balanced mood. Unfortunately, TV watching over the long term seems to be related to problems: watching television more than two hours per day and eating while watching television are both associated with obesity (60 percent of people in the United States are obese) and exacerbate risk factors for cardiovascular disease, cancer, and diabetes. It was also shown that after the initial two hours, each extra hour of television that kids watch per day is associated with an 8 percent increase in developing depressive symptoms by young adulthood. Although many people report lack of time as a major barrier to regular exercise, the average American adult spends more than four hours per day watching television.

Analysis of more than thirty years of national data shows that spending time watching television may contribute to viewers' happiness in the moment, but the long-term effects are not good. In these studies, participants reported that on a scale from 0 (dislike) to 10 (greatly enjoy), TV watching was nearly an 8. Despite the favorable rating, it seems that the enjoyment from TV is very short lasting and gives way to discontent. What was found is that unhappy people glue themselves to the television 30 percent more than happy people do. These results held even after taking into account education, income, age, and marital status. This data from nearly thirty thousand adults led the authors of this study to conclude that

> TV doesn't really seem to satisfy people over the long haul the way that social involvement or reading a newspaper does. We looked at 8 to 10 activities that happy people engage in, and for each one, the people who did

the activities more—visiting others, going to church, all those things—were more happy. TV was the one activity that showed a negative relationship. Unhappy people did it more, and happy people did it less. The data suggest to us that the TV habit may offer short-run pleasure at the expense of long-term malaise.

In the words of T. S. Eliot, "The remarkable thing about television is that it permits several million people to laugh at the same joke and still feel lonely." In short, happy people do not watch a lot of TV.

* * *

So, this chapter discussed what your grandmother already knew: that good sleep, good food, exercise, and getting out into the sun are very healthy and that stress and too much TV are not so good. What I hope came through in this chapter is that these basic concepts have strong research behind them and hold promise to treat even the most difficult depression issues. My vision for the future treatment of depression is to make each of these a priority item to be checked by every doctor and worked with by every depression sufferer to the best of his or her ability. Even if each person trying to feel better can achieve some improvement in just one or two areas, this will go a long way toward a better mood.

4

Checking Out Your Engine
and Cooling the Fire

Emotions play out in the theatre of the body.

—Antonio Damasio

You are probably getting the idea that depression is almost never caused by just one event or problem in the body; it's caused by multiple factors. At its most simplistic, you can narrow these factors down to two causes: external and internal. Using a car analogy, the external problems are like bad gasoline, a lead foot, or harsh weather and road conditions, all of which can wreck a good car over time. Internal problems are like car parts that just are not working well due to manufacturer error. Complicating this scenario, it's clear that physical external problems will make internal issues—such as mood—become more apparent, and mood problems then contribute to physical problems.

Chapter 3 talked about what we can do to change some of the key lifestyle factors that contribute to depression. Such lifestyle changes work by shifting your brain and body physiology—the external and internal factors mentioned in the car analogy—to help them heal and repair.

Chapter 4 is dedicated solely to the physical processes that contribute to depression. However, these are often not outwardly visible. The problems we will discuss here are not as obvious as, say, constipation, so they require some explanation. This chapter gives you the knowledge to identify and address issues that you, and possibly your doctor, may not know are affecting you.

BLOOD TESTS

In chapter 2, I gave you a list of blood tests to ask your physician to run for you. These tests are designed to check on factors that may be affecting your mood. Any of these can be crucial to helping your mood improve. Read on to understand the reasons for the specific tests and what you can do based on the results.

Tests: Fasting Blood Sugar and Serum Insulin

I first met my wife, Pina, in 1997 in the psychiatric medicine halls of the National Institute of Mental Health in Bethesda, Maryland. There, we researched how stress affects the brain and hormonal system. One of the first things I noticed about Pina when we were first dating was that, for an otherwise happy and positive person, if we waited too long for a dinner table at a restaurant, her mood became very irritable, somewhat difficult, and then negative. This is because when blood sugar drops or bounces up and down, it stresses the body out and can create low mood.

While many people (like my wife) can have transient mood problems if they haven't eaten, some people who tend to have low blood sugar may have hypoglycemia. People with hypoglycemia are known to be at greater risk for depression. A 2008 study from Johns Hopkins University watched intensive care patients and noticed that those with blood sugar hovering under 60 (normal is 70 to 100) had a 360 percent risk of depression when researchers checked in three months later.

Even when people eat well and often enough, sometimes they can have low blood sugar because their insulin levels are too high. Insulin is the hormone that transports the glucose absorbed from the sugar or carbohydrates you eat into your blood cells. Insulin is also responsible for storing fat and causing inflammation in the body and the brain. As we discussed in the previous chapter, inflammation in the brain can cause depression.

People with hyperglycemia (high blood sugar) or high insulin levels are also predisposed to depression. A study of adults in their late twenties and early thirties showed that when blood sugar or insulin was high, chances of depression rose 150 to 200 percent.

I recommend running blood sugar tests because knowing your fasting blood sugar and insulin levels helps you make better choices about how you eat, how you exercise, and what supplements you take to help your mood.

If you suffer from mood issues and blood sugar difficulties, I recommend checking your blood sugar on your own throughout the day for one or two days. Please download the Blood Sugar Monitor chart provided on my website (www.drpeterbongiorno.com/happybloodsugar) to help track when you eat, what you eat, your activities, and your blood sugar levels. If you have a new glucose meter, or if you do not know if your meter is accurate, talk to your pharmacist and have it calibrated. You can also bring it with you to a blood test—after the phlebotomist tests your blood, you can check your own blood sugar with your monitor and compare the results.

The benefit of checking your blood sugar is to see if it is too low or too high during regular time periods of your day. While anyone can have occasional fluctuations, people who are experiencing levels too high or low will be predisposed to mood issues. If this is you, the information below will be an especially important part of your treatment to health.

How to Treat Unbalanced Blood Sugar

I recommend the following tips for patients who experience blood sugar levels dropping below 70, elevating above 120 when they have not eaten for eight hours or above 200 at any point after eating, or if their blood tests show that insulin levels are too high:

- Eat breakfast. This simple step has been shown to help people stay happier during the day.

- Eat small, frequent meals, up to five times a day.

- Avoid all simple flour and carbohydrate foods (bread, cookies, pasta, cake).

- Alternate strength training and cardiovascular exercise six days per week.

- Take 400 mcg of chromium per day with food.

- Sprinkle a half teaspoon of cinnamon on your food once each day.

Doing these actions for as little as a week can help poor mood caused by low or high blood sugar. Anxious and irritable people tend to calm down, and depressed people often perk up.

People who have hyperglycemia may also have diabetes, and diabetic patients are known to have vastly higher rates of depressive illness. If you have high blood sugar or diabetes, stabilizing your blood sugar is crucial to treating depression and mood issues.

Test: Chemistry Panel

A chemistry panel (also known as a chem panel) is basically a shotgun test to look at many aspects of your physiology. It takes a snapshot of what is happening with your lungs, liver, and kidneys as well as gauges levels of calcium, protein, and electrolytes. If the results are abnormal in any of these categories, talk with your doctor about working on the underlying problems. Abnormalities with any of the organ systems related to these levels can cause symptoms that contribute to depressive illness. Every comprehensive blood test should include a chemistry panel.

Test: Lipid Panel

If you thought cholesterol when you read that header, you were right. A lipid panel basically checks the fasting baseline levels of the fats running around in your blood. Cardiologists and primary doctors usually check these to make sure they are not too high, but I want you to check them to make sure they are not too low. Let me explain.

I have seen low total cholesterol play a role in many depression cases. Although your psychiatrist or cardiologist may not be thinking about this, the research is very clear. Cholesterol is an important mood molecule for two reasons: it helps produce your steroid hormones, and it helps your brain recognize and use serotonin. As the parent of many important molecules in your body, cholesterol is the precursor to all steroid hormones, including glucocorticoids (for blood sugar regulation), mineralocorticoids (which maintain mineral balance and blood pressure regulation), and sex hormones (which have a strong role in mood, as we will discuss). It seems likely that low cholesterol may restrict the availability of steroidal compounds for your body. Maintaining normal cholesterol levels is also important for the function of the receptors in the brain that recognize serotonin.

A Statin Island of Woe?

While antidepressants are the most prescribed drugs in America, cholesterol-lowering medications are the number one money-making medication in this country—and around the world. In the marketed interest of saving more hearts, the cut-off range for high cholesterol has been lowered in the last few years, allowing more prescriptions. However, mounting medical research tells us that the more we lower cholesterol, the worse our mood can get.

Known as statins, cholesterol medications work by blocking a key enzyme involved in the body's production of cholesterol. Lab tests have shown that statin medication significantly disturbs the structure and function of serotonin cell receptors. When researchers added cholesterol to cells treated with statins, they came back to normal and responded to serotonin.

Other studies have suggested that statins lower needed polyunsaturated fatty acids in the brain as well. Some studies demonstrate that low postpartum levels of total cholesterol have been associated with symptoms of depression and increased relapse rates in people who have already suffered from depression.

Get Your Good Cholesterol Even Better

Low levels of high-density lipoprotein (HDL—the good cholesterol) are a known risk factor in cardiovascular disease. HDL carries bad cholesterol away from the artery walls and plays a role in toxin removal. HDL cholesterol levels are also found to be low in major depression patients and even lower in people who think about suicide. One study looked at HDL levels and mood and concluded that HDL cholesterol can be used as a marker for major depression and suicidal behavior.

How to Treat Low HDL

While conventional doctors consider low HDL to be under 40, I recommend that anyone with HDL levels under 60 work to increase them. This can be done with natural medicine treatments such as stopping smoking, exercising, and taking fish oil. Moderate alcohol consumption (one to two drinks per day) can also help increase HDL cholesterol levels. Foods that can help include oranges, dark chocolate, extra virgin olive oil, hibiscus, and black tea. The fiber supplement beta-glucan can also raise good cholesterol levels. I have a number of healthy patients with HDL levels way above 100—as of this writing, I know no reason to be concerned about high HDL levels. It seems the higher, the better.

Test: Homocysteine

Homocysteine is an independent risk factor for cardiovascular disease and a well-known marker of inflammation. Some medical professionals believe it to be a more accurate marker of inflammation than even cholesterol. The plasma level of this amino acid usually increases with age. In a large study of 3,752 men age seventy and older, an increase in homocysteine was associated with a significantly increased risk of depression. This evidence suggests that lower levels of homocysteine may decrease the incidence of depression in the elderly.

It has been found that homocysteinemia (high homocysteine in the blood) causes a decrease in S-adenosyl-L-methionine (SAMe—a compound that has been shown to help depression—more about SAMe in chapter 5). This decrease in SAMe impairs your body's ability to make neurotransmitters for the brain and negatively affects the fats and nerves of your brain. There's a strong correlation between high homocysteine and vessel damage leading to atherosclerosis, cardiovascular disease, and depressive disease. This may be why people who are depressed have high rates of cardiovascular disease, and vice versa.

The Homocysteine-Depression Connection:

High Homocysteine→Low SAMe→Low Neurotransmitters, Damaged Nerves and Vessels → Depression and Cardiovascular Disease

How to Treat High Homocysteine

There's controversy as to whether using natural therapies such as B vitamins, folic acid, and tri-methylglycine or betaine supplements is useful to lower homocysteine and ultimately protect against cardiovascular illness. However, it's clear to me that SAMe and folic acid help depression, so for anyone with high homocysteine, I typically recommend:

- SAMe: Start a dosage of 200 mg twice the first two days and then increase to 400 mg twice daily on day three, then to 400 mg three times daily on day ten, and finally to the full dose of 400 mg four times daily.

- B-complex vitamin with folate: Take B vitamin that includes 800 mcg of folate (L-5-methyltetrahydrofolate form) per day. If you are taking medications that are not effective, you may increase the folate level to 10 mg per day.

- Betaine (also called trimethylglycine): Take 3,600 mg every day.

CLINICAL CASE: MEL AND RESOLUTION, PASSION, AND HOMOCYSTEINE

A fifty-one-year-old engineer named Mel came into my office to work on a case of intractable depression. It seems about twelve years before, Mel had experienced his first bout with depression after starting a new job at an engineering firm. His work at the firm started becoming erratic—even the simple tasks of finishing paperwork became too difficult for him. As Mel described it, he tried to "hide underground" and get away from it all. At the time, he realized he was not happy with his life's work and was questioning his family life too.

Mel was prescribed Prozac, which helped his symptoms within a few weeks. He also started psychotherapy, which focused on tools to help Mel get back into the swing of work. Mel continued on the Prozac until about two months prior to our first visit, when he attempted, seemingly out of the blue to take his life. Fortunately, the attempt was unsuccessful, but the fact that his depression had returned with a vengeance was undeniable. Now his doctor had prescribed him imipramine, a medication used for severe depression.

At our first visit, I asked Mel what exactly had happened during the first bout with depression. At first he couldn't remember what it was about, for, he said, "It was so long ago, and I have not even thought of it." After I pried a bit, he remembered thinking he was saddened by a job he had "no passion for, and could not think of going there every day"—the very same feelings that prompted the recent suicide attempt.

I explained to Mel that these feelings, and this concern for the importance of his work, needed to be explored. His body had been holding on to that feeling for years, and now the pot had boiled over. This knowledge was good in a way—now Mel had an opportunity to realize his concerns and make a positive change toward enjoying his daily life. Mel didn't know what he would enjoy, so I told him he didn't need every answer right then—he just needed to start the process. When I asked what he used to enjoy, he mentioned watching his favorite baseball team and cooking chocolate chip pancakes for the kids. I helped him make a plan to schedule a baseball game and to cook breakfast one day each weekend.

I also placed Mel on a regimen of fish oils, a multiple vitamin, and acupuncture designed to help support his liver and spleen. During his initial acupuncture treatment, I burned sage and explained Native American rituals with sage (see chapter 5 for more on sage).

When Mel came back for his second visit, I noticed a faint smile and a sense of being present, something that had been missing in the first visit. Although still depressed and unable to face his work, he told me that he had thought about the need for change, and although he knew it would be hard, it was the first time he'd felt hope in a long time.

During the third visit, he complained about experiencing more anxiety and a "stuck" feeling in his stomach area, but he also reported that he'd cracked a joke with some friends and laughed heartily—something he had not been able to do in a while. At that visit, we also reviewed his completed lab tests, which included high homocysteine, low total testosterone, low normal serum carnitine, and surprisingly high vitamin D. As of this writing, I am planning on placing Mel on supplements to lower homocysteine (B_6, B_{12}, trimethylglycine, and folate) as well as 200 mg of SAMe twice a day. He will be visiting an endocrinologist for a second opinion about the testosterone level, and we will consider a testosterone transdermal patch.

I believe Mel's condition is multifaceted around his dislike for his work and his sense of being trapped at an unfulfilling job. I also see the high homocysteine, along with the low carnitine and testosterone, as a sign that his body has been primed for strong depression, and as we work to balance those physiologic factors, he should be much more resilient to depression.

Test: C-Reactive Protein

Similar to homocysteine, C-reactive protein (CRP) is a blood test that records the level of a protein that is increased in your blood when the immune system is fighting a war, a war that beats up your arteries and your nervous system and causes depression and cardiovascular disease.

When your CRP is high, it means the war is raging and your mood is losing. High CRP levels have been shown to be quite related to depression in both men and women.

How to Treat High CRP

- Exercise: Start with walking for thirty minutes three times a week and increase.

- Reduce intake of highly cooked food: Chemicals called advanced glycation end products (with the appropriate acronym, AGES) from foods that are cooked at high temperatures increase CRP levels. Eating more raw and minimally cooked foods (boiled or poached) helps.

- Take fiber and psyllium seed husk: The first place to put out the inflammatory fire is in your digestive tract, for about 80 percent of your immune system resides there. Like using an extinguisher's foamy contents to douse a fire, regular intake of quality fiber calms the inflammation in your gut and allows the residual contents to be whisked away. I recommend 25 g of total fiber for the day. You can get about 5 g by mixing a teaspoon of psyllium seed husk in eight ounces of water. Do this twice a day, in the morning and evening. Consume the rest of your daily fiber by eating quality fruits, vegetables, and flax meal throughout the day.

- Take fish oil: One teaspoon per day balances inflammation in the body.

- Take vitamin C: Swallow 500 mg three times a day to reduce elevated CRP.

- Take vitamin E: Aim for 1,200 IU every day.

Test: Complete Blood Count and Iron Panel

A complete blood count (CBC) looks at the health of your red and white blood cells. Red blood cells carry your oxygen around your body to keep your tissues alive, your energy up, and your mood strong. White blood cells form the army that is your immune system. When there are not enough red blood cells carrying oxygen, depression can result.

Iron is also important, for it helps your blood cells carry oxygen. Even if your red blood cell count is fine, if your iron is low, you will still feel fatigued. If you are predisposed to depression, low iron could be enough to cause you to become clinically depressed.

The Term Anemia Applies to Anyone Who Has

- Low red blood cells
- Low hemoglobin (the molecule within red blood cells that carries oxygen)
- Low blood iron (serum iron) or storage (ferritin)

Anemia can be debilitating and has been shown to contribute to lost work, decreased physical and emotional well-being, and interference with the ability to think clearly. All of these can lead to anxiety and depression. Do any of these symptoms describe you?

One study looked at 134 very fatigued women, most of whom had low ferritin (iron storage). The researchers split these volunteers into two groups: one group received iron supplementation while the other received a placebo (which was an inert substance without iron) daily for four weeks. None of the women knew which supplement they were receiving. In the iron group, the level of fatigue after one month decreased 29 percent versus only 13 percent in the placebo group.

Although the iron group benefit was double over the control, 71 percent of the women in the iron group did not improve. There were likely other issues affecting those women—perhaps blood sugar was one other factor. We must remember that in most cases of fatigue and depression, more than one issue needs fixing. For 29 percent of the women, iron was likely the sole issue; for the other 71 percent, other things we talk about in this book probably needed work too. Still, achieving a nearly 30 percent improvement was pretty good given that only one recommendation was given. That is about the same rate of benefit as antidepressant medications.

When serum iron and ferritin are low, it's best to talk to your doctor about possible reasons for this. In men and non-menstruating women, it's especially important. Sometimes, improper bleeding within in the body (from an ulcer, for example) can cause this and should be looked into. If the iron and iron storage are simply low due to poor intake or absorption of iron, then a supplement is appropriate.

How to Treat Low Iron

I usually recommend a patient start with 25 mg of iron per day, taken with food. Then increase to 25 mg three times per day with food. Iron succinate or fumarate forms are generally gentler on the stomach than other forms. Also, take 500 mg of vitamin C with the iron for best absorption. Finally, in some cases, I recommend taking the herbs nettles and yellow dock for best iron support and absorption effects. Nettles and yellow dock can be purchased in pills, teas, or tinctures at a health food store; follow the doses on the product you buy. Food sources of iron include grass-fed beef, dark turkey meat, and dark, leafy greens. Cooking in an iron skillet can provide some iron too.

CLINICAL CASE: WINNIE WITH LOW IRON STORAGE

When I was a student clinician in my third year of medical school, one of the first patients I had the honor of following for the summer was "Winnie," a young woman in her early thirties. I was a secondary clinician at the time, which basically meant I was allowed to listen in while the primary student clinician, who was a year ahead of me in school, asked all the questions.

Winnie was a journalist who came in for premenstrual cramps that had worsened over the past few months to the point of making it difficult to complete her work duties. During our hour-long intake of questions, we learned that Winnie had been taking Prozac for about a year to combat depression, which seemed to rear its ugly head mostly around the time of her period. Her gynecologist had prescribed the medication, suggesting that it would help her mood. Her mood did improve, but for some reason, her premenstrual periods got worse and worse. When reviewing the case with our supervising doctor, he explained to us that from a naturopathic perspective, it was common to see new symptoms pop up when another symptom is being suppressed. It's kind of like when you try to stuff too many balls in a bucket—when you try to put the lid on, one or two will pop out. In this case, Winnie's mood was pushed under the surface, but her period symptoms popped up and out.

Our supervising doctor recommended we run some blood tests, and while most of her test results were quite healthy and balanced, Winnie's ferritin was abysmally low. We started her on an iron supplement, and after one month, she reported feeling so good that her energy had even improved, though she hadn't even known it was a problem beforehand. She also mentioned her exercise seemed much stronger. Best of all, her mood had improved. After two months, her premenstrual symptoms had disappeared and she had discontinued the Prozac with no negative effects on mood.

Test: Thyroid

The thyroid test looks at how your thyroid functions. Besides its importance in mood, your thyroid is a key factor in your ability to burn food as energy, to have good bowel movements, and even to keep bad cholesterol (LDL) in check. Low thyroid function is very common. According to the American Association of Clinical Endocrinologists, one in ten Americans suffers from thyroid disease and almost half of these remain undiagnosed. Many experts suspect the heavy metal pollution and radioactive by-products from nuclear power plants may be increasing the incidence of thyroid disease. Low thyroid symptoms include weight gain, slowed thinking, memory problems, feeling cold, and constipation. Often, low thyroid can be an early or even first symptom of oncoming depression.

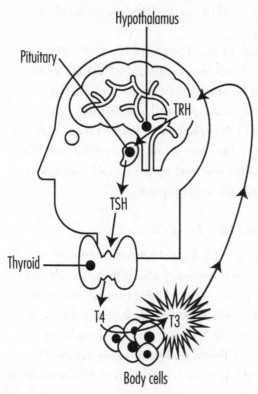

Figure 2: The Hypothalamic-Pituitary-Adrenal Axis

The blood tests I recommend look at how the brain instructs the thyroid and how well the thyroid responds to those instructions. These are Thyroid Stimulating Hormone (TSH) and the thyroid hormones thyroxine (T4) and triiodothyronine (T3). TSH is made by the pituitary gland, in the base of the brain. TSH tells the thyroid how much thyroid hormone (mostly in the form of T4) should be produced. That T4 travels to nearly all cells of the body, and gets converted to T3, which is the active form of the hormone. T4 is identical to the molecule they use to make thyroid replacement hormone. The brain has an area called the hypothalamus, which keeps track of how much T4 and T3 is present in your body, and sends a signal to the pituitary in the form of thyroid releasing hormone (TRH). The TRH in turn tells the pituitary how much TSH to make. This system is called a negative feedback loop.

In the blood stream, T4 and T3 can either actively create an effect (called the "free" form) or not (called the "bound" form). This is why it is a good idea to ask your doctor for both free and total measurements of T4 and T3 as well as something called Thyroid Binding Globulin (TBG). Sometimes your total amounts can be normal, but the active free form is low. The liver puts out this protein called TBG, which will bind up the thyroid hormones in your blood and not allow them to be active.

How to Treat Abnormal TSH, T3, or T4

If your TSH is greater than 2.5, I usually recommend patients run what is called a thyroid antibody panel. This panel helps you determine if your thyroid is malfunctioning because your immune system is attacking it (a condition called Hashimoto's disease or thyroiditis). Some doctors say 2.5 is just fine for thyroid, but the American Association of Clinical Endocrinologists has been lowering the threshold of TSH. If yours is near the new 3.0 threshold, it should be checked.

If the results show an autoimmune thyroid condition, please refer to the following section in this chapter on digestive and anti-inflammatory work.

If there's no autoimmune condition and

- TSH is above 2.2 and T4 is low but T3 is in normal range: Eat extra kelp and seaweed every day and take a thyroid glandular support, 200 mcg of selenium per day, and 300 mg of tyrosine per day.

- T3 and T4 are both low: Work with a naturopathic physician to start on a low dose of natural thyroid replacement like Armour Thyroid or Nature-Throid. These are made from dried pig thyroid. Most standard endocrinologists do not work with natural thyroid replacements because they are concerned that the amount of thyroid hormone is not identical in every batch.

Experience tells me that it's relatively uniform and patients generally do quite well on it. A good low starting dose is 15 mg per day. Your doctor should check your pulse and symptoms before starting, and then recheck you once a week to see how you feel. She should also take blood tests every few weeks to recheck your thyroid levels.

- If natural thyroid replacement is not helping you feel better, you can try a more standard synthetic thyroid replacement such as thyroxine (which is T4). This synthetic replacement is an identical molecule to what your body uses, so the chances of side effects are minimal when used at the proper dosage. With any thyroid replacement, you and your doctor should watch for palpitations and heart racing, increased temperature, excessive sweating, or weight loss. I prefer using the natural thyroid or giving T3 because it has been shown to be more helpful in depression (see the next section and chapter 7 for more on T3).

- If only T3 is low: Consider working with a doctor for a prescription of Cytomel, which is pure active T3. You can start with 5 mcg each morning and continue to increase by 5 mcg every three days until you feel well. Do not increase your dosage above 125 mcg. If you are over fifty-five years of age, cap your dosage at 60 mcg. Reasons to discontinue or lower your dosage would be if you feel a racing heart, excessive sweating, shakiness, anxiety, or fast-paced thought patterns.

- If your free T4 and T3 amounts are low, but your total amounts are normal and you have a high TBG, then you will want to consider using a detoxification plan (see chapter 4), which should include plenty of foods to help clear the liver, such as extra fiber, beets, dandelion, artichoke, kale and taking liver supportive herbs like milk thistle.

Note: If you complete the above tests and therapies and still sense your thyroid is not balanced, you may want to ask your practitioner or endocrinologist for a TRH stimulation test. With this test, a form of TRH is injected in the blood, directly stimulating the pituitary gland. If there is a problem with the pituitary, this test should be able to help identify it. Before the TSH test became more sensitive, this test was more commonly used by the medical community. This test may help you understand even better how to use various forms of thyroid support.

Test: Parathyroid

The parathyroid glands are four pea-sized organs inside the thyroid gland. Primary hyperparathyroidism (over-functioning thyroid gland) will show a high PTH number. This is frequently accompanied by high blood calcium and a low vitamin D status. The body tries to suppress intake of vitamin D in order to reduce the level of calcium in the blood, and low vitamin D alone can cause significant depression. Depressive disorders and low mood usually normalize after treatment of hyperparathyroidism. If your parathyroid and calcium are high, see an endocrinologist for best treatment options to lower parathyroid activity.

Tests: DHEA and DHEA-S

Related to testosterone, dehydroepiandrosterone (DHEA) and dehydroepiandrosterone-sulfate (DHEA-S) are molecules produced by the adrenal gland. Low DHEA-S levels are correlated with depression severity. Levels decrease with age and psychological stressors, and as DHEA goes south, mood can deteriorate. DHEA can protect against the adverse effects of stress, especially the ravages of the stress hormone cortisol. Like exercise, DHEA can increase the hippocampus nerve growth as it protects new nervous tissue from being destroyed by stress hormones.

There are two ways to measure DHEA—by looking at serum DHEA and also at DHEA-S. DHEA may be a more accurate assessment of proper hormone levels than DHEA-S, so I rely more on DHEA levels to suggest supplementation. DHEA is nonprescription over-the-counter hormonal therapy.

A number of studies report that DHEA supplementation benefits brain health and has direct antidepressant effects. DHEA can be especially effective for midlife-onset minor and major depression. A well-designed six-year study published in the *Archives of General Psychiatry* in 2005 looked at twenty-three men and twenty-three women aged forty-five to sixty-five years with midlife-onset major or minor depression. Some patients were given 90 mg of DHEA every day for the first three weeks, while other patients received a sugar pill. Those who took DHEA treatment had a 50 percent or greater reduction in depression. The treatment with DHEA was well tolerated and helped both men and women.

How to Treat Low DHEA

Though many studies have used 50 to 450 mg every day in divided doses, I recommend starting with lower doses of 5 to 15 mg every day, checking blood levels every two to three weeks. If mood does not improve or if the level of hormone does not increase, then you can increase your dosage in increments of 5 mg while monitoring with blood tests.

DHEA levels should always be checked before starting supplementation. Taking too much for your body can cause problems by increasing levels of other hormones like testosterone and estrogen. Too much DHEA in women may cause male hormone-like skin effects (greasy skin and hair, acne, itchy scalp, hair loss, or facial and body hair, especially along the midline of the lower abdomen). Men with prostate cancer or benign prostatic hyperplasia (BPH) should check with their doctor before starting DHEA.

The only known food source for DHEA is the wild yam, but its levels are way too low to have a clinical effect.

Test: Testosterone

Testosterone is the hormone most associated with being male—however, both men and women need it to maintain a good mood. Low testosterone levels may cause flattened mood, low sex drive, loss of motivation, fatigue, and general loss of well-being in both women and men. This condition has been underdiagnosed due to the nonspecific symptoms that may appear identical to clinical depression and should be tested in anyone with depression symptoms.

How to Treat Low Testosterone

Although oral versions of testosterone replacement are available, I recommend a transdermal patch to avoid interference by the liver. Anything you ingest goes through the liver, and when the liver sees all this extra hormone taken orally, it tries to bind it up by sending out a protein called sex hormone binding globulin (SHBG), which may block other hormones from working so well.

Studies show that it is safe for men to use antidepressants together with transdermal testosterone. Interestingly, it has been shown that selective serotonin reuptake inhibitors (SSRIs), the most commonly prescribed antidepressant medication, can cause infertility by lowering testosterone and sperm levels. So if a depressed man with normal serotonin but low testosterone is given an SSRI, it may make his depression even worse while also decreasing his chances of having children.

Too much testosterone can cause excess body and facial hair, acne, and may exacerbate prostate cancer risk, although newer studies are suggesting it may not be a risk to the prostate at all. Testosterone replacement should be monitored by a doctor using blood tests and checking for signs of excess.

Test: Estrogen and Progesterone

Estrogen and progesterone are well known to factor into mood both from moment to moment and as hormonal change occurs over the years. While some women may have mood issues without necessarily having imbalances in estrogen and progesterone, these are worth checking. We will discuss estrogen and progesterone further in chapter 8.

Test: Celiac Panel

Paralleling the increased intake of more bread and grain products in the past fifty years is a dramatic rise in the incidence of celiac disease—a strong inflammatory reaction to the gluten component of wheat, spelt grains, or amaranth. According to a 2004 panel at the National Institutes of Health, estimates suggest that one in one hundred people is affected, although the disease is considerably underdiagnosed.

There's a correlation between celiac disease and gluten sensitivity with mood disorder in adults and behavioral issues in both children and adults. Twenty percent of patients with celiac have overt psychiatric problems. But celiac disease holds greater risks than mood problems—undiagnosed disease has a fourfold increased risk of death.

One way you can learn if celiac disease is affecting your health and mood is to have a celiac panel as part of your next blood test. A celiac panel is composed of four tests: antigliadin antibodies IgG, antigliadin antibodies IgM, tissue transglutaminase (TTG), and secretory IgA. Together, these tests can help identify immune reactions to gluten. Although the panel is not perfect, it typically has an 80 to 90 percent accuracy rate. Accuracy can be improved by eating gluten products regularly a few weeks before the panel to ensure antibodies show up if you are producing them. The alternative gold-standard test for celiac disease is quite invasive: a biopsy of the small intestine's jejunum section, which I do not recommend unless your doctor believes there are digestive issues that warrant it.

The last test of the panel is secretory IgA. IgA stands for immunoglobulin A, which is an antibody needed to protect against infections in the mucous membranes lining the mouth, respiratory tube, and digestive tract. About 3 percent of the population is IgA deficient, suffering from a mild genetic issue that lowers this antibody. Low IgA can lead to problems with digestion and the intestinal environment. Regarding our discussion, if a person is IgA deficient, then the other celiac tests may show up falsely negative, even if they actually have celiac disease. So if your IgA is low, you may need to work further on creating a healthier digestive tract (see the "Digestive Work" section later in this chapter), and then retest for celiac disease afterward.

How to Treat Celiac Disease

Simply stated, if you have celiac disease, it's best to avoid all gluten proteins. These appear in wheat, spelt, and amaranth products. Gut linings can heal in three to six months after altering your diet—and in my experience, mood issues can improve within as little as two weeks. Most other grains like rice, quinoa, and millet are perfectly fine to eat. I recently noticed that Gino's, a well-known pizzeria in my hometown, now serves gluten-free crust. A large sign advertises this—quite a testament to the number of people who are finding gluten to be problematic in their diets.

A note about gluten allergy versus sensitivity: While people who have positive celiac tests should absolutely avoid gluten, I have seen clinically that many people who do not have a positive blood test are still obviously gluten sensitive, meaning this protein can cause inflammation in the body and contribute to mood issues even though the intestines are not overtly damaged and the celiac test was not positive.

While relatively scarce in our food supply a few hundreds years ago, now it is hard not to find gluten in some form in most of our everyday foods. Besides appearing in breads, it is used as a filler for many other foods, including imitation meats. Gluten grains are also used in animal feed, which is passed on to us when we eat the animals. As mentioned, many people who are celiac negative could still be sensitive to gluten. If you think this could be you, it is worth doing a trial of four weeks without gluten to see if your mood improves. Some people who are extra sensitive to gluten may need to stop eating it by weaning off slowly. Like a drug addiction, sometimes when you stop gluten too quickly, you can have withdrawal effects, which could temporarily make your mood feel worse.

Test: Serum Carnitine

Carnitine (affectionately known as L-3-hydroxy-4-N,N,N-trimethyl-aminobutyrate in the medical world) is an amino acid cofactor that serves to help turn fats into energy. Carnitine may play a neuropro-tective role in mood by acting as an antioxidant and an anti-inflam-matory. The supplement form of carnitine, called L-carnitine, has been shown to help mood, fatigue, and depression in patients with cancer.

How to Treat Low Carnitine

Generally speaking, L-carnitine supplementation has an enhanced effect on energy level. I recommend 500 mg of carnitine twice a day, preferably not taken with food for best absorption. I also would recheck carnitine blood levels in six weeks to look for improvement. If there's no improvement, then you can increase the dose up to 3,000 mg per day and consider more digestive work (see next sec-tion), to help you absorb your nutrients better. Levels of 3,000 mg per day have not shown any toxicity.

The word *carnitine* comes from the Latin word *carne*, which means "meat." The highest concentrations of carnitine are found in red meat. Other high concentrations are found in dairy products. Some lesser natural sources of carnitine include nuts and seeds, and smaller amounts in legumes, vegetables, and grains.

Tests: Serum Folic, B₁₂, and MTHFR Gene Variant

The word *folate* comes from the Latin word *folium*, which means "leaf," for it was realized a long time ago that there was plenty of this nutrient in leafy greens. Known for preventing neurologic defects in newborns, folic acid also plays a strong role in the production of the neurotransmitters norepinephrine and epineph-rine as well as the feel-good chemical prostaglandin. Folic acid is also needed to support dopamine production, while vitamin B_{12} is known to help in the synthesis of serotonin. There's some evidence that people with depression respond better to drug treatment if they have higher levels of vitamin B$_{12}$ and folic acid (see chapter 7).

Asian population studies suggest that people who eat traditional Chinese diets rich in folate (from healthy portions of green vegetables) have high serum folate concentrations and tend to have very low lifetime rates of major depression.

Folic acid deficiency has been noted among people with depression, and some estimates show as high as 33 percent of depressed individuals are folate deficient. Poor diet, alcohol, antiepileptic medications, and birth control pills can all contribute to folate deficiency.

Some people have a genetic inability to convert the typical folic acid into L-methylfolate, the form the body uses. The methyltetrahydrofolate reductase (MTHFR) gene variant test is a blood test to determine if you have that genetic inability.

How to Treat Low Folic Acid or B$_{12}$

Oral doses of both folic acid (800 mcg–15 mg daily) and vitamin B$_{12}$ (1 mg daily) should be tried to improve treatment outcome in depression. B vitamins like folic acid and B$_{12}$ are water soluble and generally safe.

If the MTHFR gene variant test suggests your ability to convert folic acid is challenged, you can bypass this problem by supplementing with the L-methylfolate form of folic acid.

Avoid folic acid if you are taking seizure medication or methotrexate for cancer, as it can block the effects. However, folate has been found to be liver protective for patients using methotrexate to treat rheumatoid arthritis (RA) without blocking its general effect.

Even if your levels of B$_{12}$ and folic acid are normal, it may still be prudent to supplement with extra B$_{12}$ and folic acid if other treatments, including medications, are not working. It's quite possible that you may have a deficiency in your body tissue while still showing reasonable levels in the blood.

Excellent food sources of folate are spinach, asparagus, romaine lettuce, turnip greens, mustard greens, calf's liver, collard greens, cauliflower, broccoli, parsley, lentils, and beets. Excellent sources of B_{12} are snapper and calf's liver. Other sources of vitamin B_{12} include venison, shrimp, scallops, salmon, and beef. Vegetarian sources have significantly lower available B_{12}, and the best of these are sea plants (like kelp), algae (like blue-green algae), brewer's yeast, tempeh, miso, and tofu.

Test: Serum 25 (OH) Vitamin D

Most people associate vitamin D with healthy bones, but it also plays a central role in mood—to the point that some experts have dubbed it "the happy vitamin." Vitamin D deficiency has also been connected to conditions like autoimmune and cardiovascular diseases, cancers, and chronic pain. One large study published in the *Archives of Internal Medicine* suggests that all causes of death may be lowered by giving supplemental vitamin D. Everyone who is breathing should have this vitamin checked.

Low levels of vitamin D are likely involved in depression in several ways. Vitamin D affects nerve growth factor, a molecule in the body that helps nervous tissue grow and repair. It's hard to have good mood without that repair mechanism. Vitamin D also helps produce serotonin, testosterone, and thyroid hormone. There's also an increase of depressive symptoms in adults whose mothers had low vitamin D while they were pregnant with them. Furthermore, many cells in the brain's center, called the hypothalamus, respond to vitamin D. The hypothalamus is responsible for some main controls of how the nervous system, hormones, and stress system work together. This system is called the hypothalamic-pituitary-adrenal axis and is most often imbalanced in depression.

Many studies show the benefits of vitamin D for mood problems. In a large study of one thousand older adults, mean levels of vitamin D were low in those with minor and major depression compared with controls. A smaller study focused on forty-four healthy participants in winter, when vitamin D levels are low. They were randomly assigned to five days of treatment with 400 or 800 IU of vitamin D$_3$ or placebo. Compared with the placebo group, both doses of the vitamin increased positive mood and decreased negative mood. A Norwegian study of 441 overweight people measured vitamin D levels. Those below 40 nmol/L (16 mg/dL) were shown to be more depressed. These subjects were then given 20,000 IU or 40,000 IU or placebo once a week. Those given 40,000 IU experienced a 33 percent reduction in depression levels, those given 20,000 IU had a 20 percent reduction, and the placebo group reported a 5 percent decrease.

The main food source of vitamin D is fish. Most people believe the healthy fats in fish can prevent depression, but given what you just read, you may decide it's the vitamin D.

Although there are a few forms of vitamin D in the body that can be tested, the test indicative of true vitamin D status is 25-hydroxy (OH) vitamin D. Make sure your doctor runs that exact one.

How to Treat Low Vitamin D

Normal levels of vitamin D range from 30 to 100. An ideal level of vitamin D is around 50. The most natural way to get vitamin D is to expose some bare skin to the sun. As we discussed in chapter 3, some sun is very healthy, and unless you have a high risk of skin cancer, it's a good idea to absorb sun until the point you start to get a little bit red. Food such as salmon, eggs, dairy, and butter have the most vitamin D, but may not be enough to raise levels. A general guideline I use to start supplemental vitamin D$_3$ is to take 2,000 IU per day for each 10 units you would like to raise your levels. So, if your vitamin D level is 20 and you would like to raise it to 50, then 6,000 IU per day would be adequate. It's best to check blood levels one month after starting supplementation and adjust accordingly.

Research demonstrates that dosages of 4,000 IU of vitamin D per day in depressed patients tend to improve well-being, so if you do not know your levels, this may be a good and safe place to start. In a clinical setting, weekly doses of 50,000 IU intramuscular are available. Although no long-term studies have reviewed this method from a natural perspective to date, it seems like a less natural way to present this vitamin to the body, for the body would not usually take in so much at one time. Studies of patients given long-term oral treatment of 14,000 IU per day seemed to have no toxicity and did show significantly decreased depression relapse rates.

Because vitamin D is fat soluble and can build up to toxic levels in your system—leading to high calcium in the blood, kidney issues, and excessive bone loss—it's advisable to run lab tests before taking this vitamin. Prudent research suggests that your blood levels should not exceed 100 ng/mL, but the exact amount of vitamin D required to induce toxicity is unknown and is probably a different number for each person. One researcher suggested in 1999 that this amount is 20,000 IU per day. However, many cases have administered much higher doses without side effects or toxicity. One recent meta-analysis looked at ordinary doses of 400 to 800 IU per day of long-term vitamin D supplementation and did not seem to be associated with any adverse effects.

There's contrasting information as to whether supplementing with the forms of vitamin D_2 (ergocalciferol) or D_3 (cholecalciferol) is optimal. Plants manufacture vitamin D_2, whereas vitamin D_3 is synthesized by humans in the skin when it's exposed to UVB rays from sunlight. My experience has been with using D_3, which seems to have a beneficial effect on blood levels and, as a result, mood. If vitamin D_3 does not seem to work for you, then you may want to try vitamin D_2.

Serum Mercury

Mercury testing is used to detect excessive amounts of mercury, which can contribute to nervous system disorders, mood disorders, and cardiovascular disease. I recommend running this test to see if there has been acute or chronic exposure to increased levels of mercury. It may also be ordered to monitor those who are regularly exposed to mercury. It does not, however, tell you if you have had an exposure of mercury that is sitting in your body tissues. I have seen high levels of mercury in patients experiencing a sudden onset of depression, so it's worth checking. We will talk more about how to treat both acute and long-term mercury and other metal poisonings later in this chapter (see "Detoxification and the Brain").

Test: ABO Blood Type and Rh

While people generally know that blood type can affect the ability to give and receive blood, relatively few people are aware that blood type suggests a tendency for a person's body to respond favorably or poorly to specific foods, even among healthy choices. Knowing your blood type can help you make better choices regarding which foods may be pro-inflammatory and which may best support your repair. More about this can be learned by reading Dr. Peter D'Adamo's book *Eat Right 4 Your Type*. I have used the blood type diet successfully in a number of cases where other dietary changes didn't work. Running the ABO blood type and Rh test allows you to pursue this work further.

DIGESTIVE WORK

It's almost cliché in the world of naturopathic care to "treat the gut" when you are working with any health issue. As cliché as it may be, this tenet of naturopathic care may be the keystone in an effective healing plan for patients with depression.

Constipation

Growing up, my brother used to tell me that if you don't poop, "your brain gets fuzzy." Although he was a youngster, he was medically accurate. Without trying to be too graphic here, it's important to remember that a good poop can really make a person feel good.

For instance, bowel movements have been linked with female self-esteem as well as with maintaining relationships. In depression, self-esteem and relationships are strong challenges. A 2001 study from the journal *Gut* compared thirty-four women between the ages of nineteen and forty-five who had suffered from constipation for five years or more with those of the same age range who had no history of constipation. It was clearly shown that the constipated women had a worse score for overall health and felt less feminine. The constipated women also found it much harder to form close relationships than those with normal bowel functioning.

Interestingly, this study also looked at rectal blood flow, which reflects the function of nerve pathways from the brain to the gut. These nerve pathways are often affected by stress. Reduced rectal blood flow was strongly associated with anxiety, depression, bodily symptoms, and impaired social skills as well as feeling unfeminine. The higher the psychologically abnormal score, the lower was the rectal blood flow.

The authors of this study concluded that a woman's psychological makeup alters the function of the involuntary nerves linking the brain to the digestive system. Reduced activity of these nerves slows gut function, resulting in constipation. Because most neurotransmitters needed for good brain mood are made in the digestive tract, slowed digestive function may play a role in how a woman feels about herself and how she responds in a relationship. Other studies have also shown higher rates of psychiatric issues with persons who have bowel problems like Crohn's disease, colitis, or irritable bowel syndrome.

Getting Things Moving

To learn the importance of good bowel movements, it makes sense to help get things moving. I often tell patients it's healthy to have a bowel movement every day. Although some medical texts recommend three times a week as normal, I believe once a day should be the minimum.

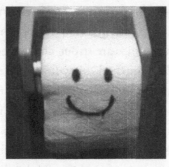

Water is the first step toward regular bowel movements. Besides helping the body absorb important amino acids, water keeps things flowing throughout the body. If we do not have enough water, the body steals it from the colon contents, making us constipated. Second, a little fiber (about 25 g a day) goes a long way for better mood—and for better relationships and self-esteem, according to the study. Add a plentiful amount of fruits and veggies to your diet. If this is not enough, sometimes flax meal, psyllium, or organic dried prunes may do the trick to, as my Great Uncle Joe used to say, "get the pipes moving." Third, stress reduction via acupuncture, meditation, yoga, or other work may help to open up bowel movement.

Serotonin and Digestion

Dubbed "the second brain" by Dr. Michael Gershon of Columbia University, the digestive tract and its accompanying bundle of nerves, called the enteric nervous system, play a major role in the production of neurotransmitters used by the brain. The nervous system around the digestive tract and the brain are very closely linked—in fact, they develop from the same embryonic tissue. And, 80 to 90 percent of the body's serotonin is produced and located in the gastrointestinal tract. Serotonin is an amine that is formed from tryptophan in the digestive tract's enterochromaffin cells (EC) and in other similar cells called enterochromaffin-like cells (ECL). Both EC and ECL are widely distributed in the gastrointestinal tract.

Tryptophan → 5-Hydroxytryptophan → Serotonin →
Better Mood

AN HONEST NOTE ABOUT SEROTONIN, RESEARCH, AND MEDICINE

There's an old joke that goes something like this: One night, a wino dropped his car keys in a mostly dark parking lot. As he was looking for them over and over in an area around the sole lamppost, some observant person came up to him and said, "Hey, friend, you could have lost your keys anywhere in this parking lot—why are you only looking over here?" The drunk man responded, "Because the light is better."

As you continue reading this book, please remember that oftentimes in medicine, we tend to search where the light is better. The truth is, it's very simplistic to put up a diagram that has the word *serotonin* pointing to good mood. If life were really so simple, antidepressant medications like Prozac and Zoloft that increase serotonin levels would work 100 percent of the time. In this book, I tend to discuss certain factors like serotonin because those are included in available research at this time—and honestly, much of this research is likely driven by the need to sell drugs. The research is not perfect, but we can learn from it as long as we keep it in perspective as a part of the whole picture.

The delicate process of converting tryptophan, the amino acid which converts to 5-hydroxytryptophan and ultimately to serotonin, is vulnerable to malabsorption problems in the digestive tract, in which the body does not absorb the nutrients we eat. If food we eat irritates the EC, the digestive "brain" sees that as a possible poison. It reacts by pouring out large amounts of serotonin to increase movement so the gut empties and everything is cleared out. This may be why many people with mood disorders as well as those with high stress experience accompanying diarrhea.

Celiac Disease and Mood

As we discussed earlier in this chapter, one well-studied condition that leads to malabsorption problems is celiac disease. This is an inflammatory disease of the upper small intestine resulting from gluten ingestion in genetically susceptible individuals. The immune system reacts to gluten lectins (or proteins) and creates a war-like effect, throwing chemical bombs in the hope of destroying the proteins. This inflammation causes the lining of the small intestine to be destroyed, which leads to malabsorption of several important nutrients. Both inflammation (which can kick off inflammation in the brain) and low nutrients can lead to mood and mental instability.

One study reported a prior history of psychiatric treatment in a high proportion of adults with celiac disease, even years before diagnosis. Researchers studying the blood of untreated celiac patients found the plasma tryptophan reading to be significantly lower compared with treated and control groups. Such studies show us that abnormally low amounts of tryptophan in patients with depression and behavior disorders are a likely marker of serotonergic dysfunction due to impaired availability of tryptophan. Importantly, this can be reversed to normal in those who follow a gluten-free diet.

While gluten is the center of attention when discussing celiac disease, it is important to remember that many other foods may also create sensitivity, inflammation, and eventual malabsorption. More information about using food modulation to treat depressive disorder will be discussed later.

This book spends a fair amount of time researching the benefits of supplements. Even if you are eating a perfect blend of healthy foods, these supplements may indeed be useful because your intestines are not absorbing the nutrients from the food you are eating. Even worse, if you are eating the standard American diet, then there's no way you are even getting the nutrients you need. So supplements can help. But, it's still most vital to remember that for true healing, eating the healthy foods and fixing the digestive tract so it can absorb these foods are necessary for your long-term health.

Anti-Inflammatory Work

Even though the worlds of psychiatry and gastroenterology do not meet in conventional medical wisdom, you now know that there's a strong correlation between a digestive tract that is not working properly and poor mental health. As we just learned, malabsorption problems in the digestive tract keep you from absorbing the nutrients you need to be healthy.

But there's a second, even more heated reason why a poorly functioning digestive tract makes your mood sour. It's inflammation. The Latin word for inflammation is *inflammare*, which means "to set on fire." Inflammation is the mark of an immune system on high alert trying to get rid of an irritant or kill something it thinks does not belong—and the casualties of this war can be your brain, health, and mood. In fact, some researchers have described depression as a low-grade systemic inflammatory condition. This is why we spent time looking at inflammation markers in your blood earlier in this chapter.

When the immune system is on high alert, it chronically releases what the immunology world calls inflammatory mediators, which are cells and little chemical bombs that keep the war going. Some of these chemicals break down cell membranes and fats, some break bonds between cells, and some can even cause fever. Immune response in the digestive tract is known to lead to flu-like symptoms, fatigue, anxiety, and of course, depression.

When I researched at the National Institutes of Mental Health, part of my work was to study what inflammation could cause in the body. To do this, my research team and I gave rats regular doses of a bacterial coat compound called lipopolysaccaride (LPS). This prompted a strong inflammatory response in the animal's body. We wore masks to use LPS, for it can elicit a strong response in humans too. We studied what chronic inflammation could cause in the rats, and we found that the animals would show signs of sickness behavior—fatigue, low mood, low motivation, and other symptoms that clearly resembled depression. Similarly, overactivation of the immune system is observed in many depressed patients, and depression is more frequent in those with an overactive immune system. Furthermore, inflammation alters brain serotonin levels.

It's also important to remember that inflammation breeds inflammation—similar to how an itchy spot makes you scratch, which aggravates it and makes it more itchy.

Leaky Gut

When the digestive tract is inflamed over a long period of time, its repair mechanisms cannot keep up with this war, and the walls break down. When the walls break down, this is called gut permeability or what many people simply call "leaky gut."

If you have a predisposition to heart disease, the inflammation from leaky gut travels to your coronary arteries and causes inflammation and blockage there. If your genetic book of life has the directions for an autoimmune condition like rheumatoid arthritis, the inflammation may go to your joints and cause pain and disfigurement. People with mood disorders have a tendency toward inflammation in various parts of the brain, and if leaky gut is present, then the likelihood of the inflammation reaching the brain and causing low mood and brain degeneration is much greater than if the intestines are healthy, happy, and intact.

The Digestion-Disease Connection:

Inflamed Digestive Tract → Leaky Gut → Mood Problems, Heart Disease, Cancer, Autoimmune Disease, Etc.

The idea that digestive problems lead to depression-causing inflammation is a key concept. Much of the work I discuss, including the allergy-elimination program, blood type diet, digestive repair, and anti-inflammatory work, is based on this concept.

DETOXIFICATION AND THE BRAIN

Just as foods we are sensitive or allergic to can cause reactions in our digestive tract and lead to chronic inflammation, chemicals in our environment can also contribute to poor mood and physical problems.

Your Brain on Heavy Metals

We have long known the correlation between neurological problems and toxic chemicals—for example, the association between lead paint exposure and learning and behavior disorders in children. However, the conventional medical system does not really think about adult mood and behavior issues in relation to metal toxicity. Despite this fact, mounting information reveals that toxic exposures may accumulate over time to cause more subtle slow degeneration of brain and nervous system tissue, resulting in subtle sickness. As an example of the insidious nature of these metals, one study looked at 281 kids who had been exposed to lead and compared them to 287 non-exposed kids. The exposed children showed significantly more neuropsychiatric symptoms than average adults—but these symptoms occurred more than twenty years after their initial exposure.

The metals most frequently associated with depression are lead, mercury, and cadmium, and they are commonly found in our environment. We can trace the origins of these particular toxins to factories, dental work, welding equipment, cigarette smoke, and old galvanized water pipes. There's another source you may not expect: natural medicines such as Ayurvedic (from India) remedies and Chinese herbs have been implicated as sources (which is why it's important to purchase supplements you know are made with the highest quality).

Note: If you are not sure about a supplement's quality, ask a naturopathic physician or other like-minded practitioner who has looked into the companies and its sources and quality control for the supplements.

These sources are all around us, giving these metals easy access to our body. Once in our system, these metals tend to generate imbalances between pro- and antioxidant balance, which can lead to inflammation and neurological damage. They can destroy the function of enzymes and proteins in your body, especially the ones that contain sulfur. To give you one example of the clinical effect of these metal toxins, a review of medical literature has shown that exposure to mercury can give rise to the symptoms and traits often found in autistic people. When metals attack molecules with sulfur groups (an element found in your nerve tissue), they negatively affect the function of your nervous system in many ways. Metals can cross your blood-brain barrier, and they have an affinity for the fatty sheaths of the nerves (myelin) and the outer covering of each cell (cell membranes). They destroy the proteins in the brain (enzymes) that are responsible for reactions like communication, detoxification, and repair. Metals can also cause problems with your brain's ability to maintain proper levels of serotonin, the neurotransmitter needed for good mood.

We know inflammation from digestive imbalance can cause mood issues. Well, heavy metals and other toxic chemicals can cause brain inflammation. To make matters worse, if inflammation has already set in, your brain cells become even more vulnerable to toxins. But don't worry; the body wants to clean this up for you. We will talk about how to help the body quell the inflammation and remove the toxins in the last section of this chapter.

MSG

Have you ever heard of monosodium glutamate, also known as MSG? You may be saying to yourself, "That's the stuff in processed foods and known best for its use in Chinese restaurants. It gives some people headaches, right?" Well, if you thought that, you are correct. MSG has something called glutamate, which is, in small amounts, a neurotransmitter. In larger amounts it's a toxic by-product of brain metabolism. The brain uses a very elaborate system to remove glutamate, but mercury, aluminum, and other toxins can easily damage the proteins the brain uses to do this, thus rendering the brain cells much more easily damaged. People who can't take the MSG likely already have a buildup of glutamate.

A patient's clinical history and certain specific symptoms may help the practitioner suspect toxicity. Check the following list of the most common symptoms to see if any describe you. Certain compounds are specifically associated with disease conditions, which may clue you in as to which metal may be the culprit.

Symptoms Associated with Heavy Metals

- Tremors
- Numbness
- Tingling
- Headaches
- Confusion
- Fatigue

HEAVY METAL	ASSOCIATED ADVERSE HEALTH EFFECT
Lead	Parkinsonism, memory and thinking problems, lower IQ, learning difficulties in children
Mercury	Memory and thinking problems, mood problems, heart conditions, high blood pressure, infertility, immune dysfunction
Cadmium	Osteoporosis, kidney damage, cancer
Arsenic	Diabetes

Heavy Metals and Associated Conditions

Checking for Metals in Your Body

Finding out the levels of toxic metals in your body can be useful to help decide if working on clearing them should be an option for you. While there is no perfect way to test for these toxic compounds, I have found the following methods helpful in assessing the need to address metal toxicity.

Hair and Blood Analysis

One type of mercury called methylmercury can collect in hair, making hair testing a valuable tool, but this test may not show the burden of other types of mercury often sitting in the body.

Conventional medicine uses blood tests for heavy metals to look for overt acute exposure. What this means is if you were exposed to a lot of heavy metal a relatively short time ago, the blood tests will pick this up. But if you had a slow accumulation of metals that gradually changed your mood, the blood test will not be helpful, for the toxic metal had time to settle into your fatty tissue, like your nervous system, where it's causing the problems. As a result, checking blood for heavy metals is useful for current exposure, but does not show past exposure or total body burden.

Check Your Pee

To show whether you have metals trapped in your body tissue, a more accurate test is called a metal provocation test. This means you will first have your urine tested. Unless you have had a recent large exposure, this first urine should show very little or no metals. Then your naturopathic physician or other health care practitioner will give you a small amount of an agent called oral dimercapto-succinic acid (DMSA) or sometimes you may have an intravenous infusion of a chemical called 2,3-dimercapto-1-propanesulfonic acid (DMPS). DMSA or DMPS goes into your system and pulls out some of the metals hiding there. After you take the DMSA or DMPS, you will have your urine tested again to see if metals are indeed hiding out. Based on this test, you and your clinician will figure out the best way to clear the metals out. We will talk about some of the ways at the end of this chapter.

The Pesticide Pest

Besides the ubiquity of metals in our environment, another concern is various commonly used chemicals that may also lead to depression in susceptible people. These often hail from the use of insecticides, herbicides, and thousands of other industrial and household chemicals.

Have you ever thought about why pesticides work? They work (and work pretty well, I might add) by disrupting neurological function in the insect. A relatively large amount of pesticide kills an insect on contact. Since we humans are bigger creatures, we don't necessarily die immediately from exposure to food and environmental pest controls, but these chemicals do enter our fat and nervous tissue, and sit there over time, slowly causing trouble with our nervous, immune, and hormonal systems. Pretty much all of us have these chemicals in our system—and if you are predisposed to mood issues like depression, their presence tips the odds against you feeling good.

The Depression-Diabetes-Pesticide Connection

A 2006 article in the journal *Diabetes Care* revealed that people with diabetes have a much higher risk of being depressed—and people with depression have a much higher risk of getting type 2 diabetes. The study focused on more than two thousand people and determined that if people didn't have pesticides in their system, even if they were obese, the chances of getting diabetes were next to nothing. Let me repeat that: if there were no pesticides or herbicides found in a person—that person had virtually no risk of diabetes, even if obese! Let me ask you, did you hear about this in the news? I know I didn't—I know when there's a new drug that can help one in a thousand people, it makes news, but when breakthrough research suggests an industry practice is likely causing all cases of type 2 diabetes, this is not even discussed. Well, anyway, my point is that given the strong connection between diabetes and depression, it's not unlikely that toxic substances in our body play a strong role in the development of mood disorder.

If you would like to have a valuable, noncommercial, and free resource for information about toxicity, please see the Environmental Working Group information in the resources section at the end of this book.

HOW TO DE-INFLAME AND DETOX

Okay, this is where the rubber hits the road. You now understand the connection between an unhealthy digestive tract, food disorders, stress, inflammation, and poor mood. You also learned about the clear connection between toxic metals and chemicals that can enter your body and cause disruption of the brain, immune system, and hormonal system. So, what can you do about it?

I have divided your detoxification plan into three steps. Step 1 is to be carried out pretty much every day—it's a lifestyle change, and it will keep your body clean and happy. Step 2 is to actively remove inflammatory foods, helping your body clean out and repair the digestive tract. Step 3, if needed, is to actively clean out heavy metals and toxic burdens like pesticides that might be hampering your mood from getting better.

Step 1: Lifestyle Changes

This first step can be considered a lifetime, everyday kind of plan. For many people, even with severe issues of digestion and mood, this first step is quite effective, even by itself.

Drink Up

Drink at least 50 ounces of water a day, or about 1 ounce for every 2 pounds of body weight. For the person who is 120 pounds, that would be 60 ounces of water. If you are not sure how much you are drinking, then measure it out for a day or two to find out. I personally like to drink one or two large glasses of room temperature water in the morning, and then I carry my stainless steel 40 ounce bottle to drink during the workday. I have a little more at home in the evening. If getting up to pee at night is an issue, limit your water intake a few hours before bedtime. If possible, consider purchasing a high-quality water filter.

Bring in the Fiber

Fiber is important to clean out the body and remove inflammation. Studies of patients taking in fiber have shown dramatic decreases in CRP, the inflammatory marker we talked about earlier. Fiber is key, for it basically sucks up all the toxins, hormonal by-products, and cholesterol released by the liver. One of the liver's many jobs is to clean the blood and dispose of the junk the body has accumulated from intake of food, liquids, drugs, and so on but doesn't need. It collects this refuse and sends it through the bile ducts and into the intestines. From the intestines, the junk leaves our body. If we do not have enough fiber in the intestines to suck it up and send it out, then we end up reabsorbing it into the body. This is why cholesterol also decreases with fiber intake.

One way to know if you are taking in enough fiber is to check your poop. Healthy movement is one easy, full-diameter bowel movement per day. The better your poops, the better your brain will work.

Here are some good sources of dietary fiber:

- Organic, unsulphured prunes
- 1 cup cooked greens like kale or Swiss chard
- 2 cups fresh salad
- 1 teaspoon fine-grade psyllium in 8 ounces of water once or twice a day
- 1 to 2 tablespoons of flax meal in your cereal or on a salad
- 1 organic carrot and 1 rib of organic celery
- 1 apple a day (cliché, yes, but effective due to the wonderful pectin fiber found in apples)
- 1 cup lentil soup

A note of caution: You may not need to add all these fibers, and do not add them all at once. It really depends on your particular system what, and how much, you need, so try them slowly. I have also noticed that many patients with irritable bowel syndrome should stay away from raw foods, for sometimes these can aggravate that condition.

Move Your Body

Regular body movement is key. At minimum, walk every day for thirty minutes. Your lymphatic system is like the sewage system for your body, taking in all the sludge that will eventually be dumped out. Unlike your blood vessels, your lymphatic system does not move this fluid unless you are moving your muscles. If you don't exercise, there's no way to clear out the sludge.

Sleep It Off

As we talked about in chapter 3, sleep is crucial for a good brain function and detoxification. Remember to go to bed by eleven p.m. at the latest and to rack up at least seven and a half hours of sleep every night. If you have trouble sleeping, please revisit chapter 3 for methods to naturally help you sleep.

Step 2: Clear the Digestive Tract

Once you've made the lifestyle change detailed in step 1 and you're having daily bowel movements, you can start working on the action plan of step 2. This plan can be carried out for up to three weeks. When you remove the toxic onslaught, then your body has a better chance to heal and clean up. Using a military analogy, a country cannot put out the fires, fix, clean up, and heal effectively if it's being bombarded. It's time to stop the shelling so your body can clean up and heal.

I usually recommend my patients do this step two or three times a year.

Inflammatory Foods

If you haven't noticed, in the discussion above, I didn't tell you to stop eating this or that food. I find that when we focus on what is being taken away, most people feel deprived. So for the long term, the plan in step 1 is to include healthy foods—not so much to exclude the unhealthy ones. To detox, though, this step asks you to avoid (for three quick weeks) foods that are considered the most likely to cause inflammation.

The foods you will want to avoid include:

- Dairy and cow's milk products (rice milk, almond milk, and hemp milk are good alternatives)
- Gluten (from wheat, rye, triticale, oat, and barley)—this includes all conventionally made pasta, bagels, cupcakes, cookies, and so on (quinoa, wild and brown rice are okay)
- Soy and tofu products
- Citrus (except grapefruit and lemons)
- Peanuts (other raw nuts are fine)
- Corn products of any kind

You'll also want to add anti-inflammatory foods to your diet:

- 1 tablespoon olive oil, unheated on top of your food or salad
- Raw nuts and seeds like walnuts, sunflower seeds, or pumpkin seeds
- Organic berries, especially blueberries, raspberries, or lingonberries
- Grass-fed beef (Try to limit red meat to once a week.)
- Organic, free-range chicken
- Cold-water, low-mercury, wild fish like wild salmon, mackerel, or cod (See www.drpeterbongiorno.com/happyfish for more cold-water fish ideas.)

* * *

Look into the blood type diet for advanced information about which foods are most healthy for your body and which may be inflammatory. Ask your naturopathic physicians or other practitioners if they are trained to use blood type diet or advanced genotype diet work—using blood type diet information in a more individualized context. For more information, see Dr. Peter D'Adamo's first book, *Eat Right for your Blood Type*, which introduced this concept to the world. This book is listed in the resources section at the back.

Organic Foods

Take note of which foods in your diet are high in pesticides and switch these to organic. The foods highest in pesticides, according to the Environmental Working Group, include berries, celery, apples, peaches, nectarines, grapes, bell peppers, potatoes, kale, and collard greens. Keeping these foods organic significantly decreases the levels of pesticide in your body.

Environmental Chemicals

Try to replace your home cleaners, household chemicals, shampoo, lotion, and toothpaste with more natural versions that do not contain pesticides, herbicides, perfumes, dyes, and parabens. A good rule of thumb is that if you have not heard of the ingredient, or can't pronounce it, it's probably worth staying away from. Also, try to take off your shoes when you enter your house. Many of the heavy metals in our homes are tracked in on our shoes.

Shake It Up

A number of good-quality supplement companies now offer protein shakes with detoxification factors that can help the liver clean out, help the intestines heal, lower inflammation, and help supply amino acids for good protein levels. The increased protein serves as a support to build neurotransmitters. Some of my favorites are Mediclear by Thorne Research, UltraInflamX and UltraClear Renew by Metagenics, and Metabolic Cleanse by Douglas Laboratories. You can follow the directions on the label, and you can take one serving two to three times a day with water or rice milk. Or, if you have a blender, you can make a delicious smoothie.

Sauna

You can increase the detoxification benefit of exercise by adding a good sweat to your day four days a week for these three weeks. Plan on spending twenty minutes in the sauna—if you can find a dry sauna, this will work the best, for the dry heat pulls even more junk out of your system. The best time to go is after your exercise. Make sure you drink some water before you hit the sauna, and don't bring in a magazine—through off-gassing, these emit some of the chemicals we are trying to get rid of.

Dry Skin Brushing

The skin is a major organ of elimination. Dry skin brushing can

- Remove dead cells, which block skin pores, to allow the skin to breathe easier and increase the elimination of waste products
- Improve lymph and blood circulation in the skin and return fluids to the heart
- Transport nutrients to the skin and clear out stagnant material
- Decrease the body's circulation and elimination work load
- Warm the skin

Turmeric

You can buy this anti-inflammatory herb as a capsule, or you can cook with it as a spice. I find my patients are more consistent with the capsule version. Meriva—turmeric bound to phosphatidylcholine—is much more absorbable than regular turmeric.

Colonics

You are taking in plenty of fiber now and pooping once or twice a day, so that is sufficient. You can further help your colon clear out toxins from your body by using a colonic, if you are up to it. Colonics enhance the process because the colon sends a signal to the liver to release even more. Colonics are not painful—in fact, most patients feel revitalized afterward. I recommend one colonic a week on the seventh, fourteenth, and twenty-first days of the detox. Do not have a colonic if you are pregnant, have active bowel disease, or are bleeding in the colon or rectum.

CLINICAL CASE: MEGAN'S EMOTIONAL AND PHYSICAL DETOX

Megan was a thirty-four-year-old woman who came to see me for skin rashes and chronic vaginal yeast infections. During a patient's first visit, I always ask the question, "If I could wave a magic wand, what symptoms or situation would you like to see get better first?" She told me that even though the skin rashes were worrisome, what she really would like to do first is let go of her obsession with her former fiancé of three years, whom she had broken up with six months before. She said, "I can't get him out of my mind." She also told me that since, she had been staying home more, getting out of bed late on the weekends, and generally ignoring her concerned friends.

I suspected some depression and suggested she try a nourishing detox that would help clear her skin, clear the vaginal symptoms, and improve her mood at the same time. I had her use a protocol similar to the steps 1 and 2 detailed here, and I asked her to come in twice a week to check in and to work on her Heart/Spirit energy using acupuncture treatments. At the end of her second week, I asked her about her ex-fiancé, to which she replied "Wow, I haven't thought of that guy in about a week." Cleared of vaginal symptoms and skin rashes, Megan was dating again within the month.

Spirituality

Meditate twice a day for five to twenty minutes at a time. Do yoga. Consider journaling about both what you are grateful for and the negative ideas you would like to let go. Physical detoxing can open the door to emotionally letting go. Sometimes, an effective detox also includes releasing negative messages and thoughts that do not serve us in a healthy way.

Step 3: Flush Toxins

Step 3 should be performed over the same three weeks you do steps 1 and 2. But remember, if you are not having a bowel movement every day, only perform step 1. When you have a bowel movement, then you can add steps 2 and 3 for three full weeks.

Green Superfoods

Add chlorella and spirulina to a drink once a day. These freshwater algae are mild detoxifiers. Their fibers help bind heavy metals, pesticides, and even polychlorinated biphenyls (PCBs). PCBs are industrial chemicals that were used in electrical equipment but then banned in the 1970s; however, they're still found in the environment, and we take these in when we eat fish and inorganic butter. Green superfoods help your body release them. These green helpers contain more chlorophyll per gram than any other plant and can trap toxic metal in the digestive tract while also speeding up the cleansing of the bowel, bloodstream, and liver. Chlorella and spirulina, like most green superfood drinks, come in powders you can add to a big glass of water. I recommend starting the day by having a nice green drink with a squeeze of lemon about thirty minutes before your breakfast.

Cilantro

When you use a natural substance or chemical to remove toxic metals, it is called chelation. Cilantro is a common herb with an active component called mercaptan, which can penetrate the blood-brain barrier, find mercury, bind it, and release it into general circulation, where the liver and kidneys can help move it out of the body. So mercaptan acts as a natural and gentle chelator. Cilantro's mercaptan can change the charge on the mercury inside your cells to a neutral state and allow it to diffuse out. Cilantro also has blood sugar lowering properties and is an anti-inflammatory, antibacterial, and antioxidant. Cilantro is available as a liquid tincture or in capsules. Dosage depends on the form you purchase, so follow label directions. I do not recommend using cilantro unless you are also using a chlorella or spirulina product to make sure any released metals are ushered out of the body.

Garlic and Antioxidants

Animal studies in which subjects took garlic and antioxidants with a chelating agent were more efficient at removing toxic metals from their systems and recovered faster. If you prefer fresh garlic, eat one to two raw cloves. You can dice them and mix them with wildflower honey for palatability. If you prefer a capsule, then you can purchase a concentrated garlic extract and take about 600 mg twice a day. Please visit my website, www.drpeterbongiorno.com/happygarlic, for a 2008 comprehensive journal article I co-authored on the subject of garlic.

Multi-mineral Supplement

Take a supplement that includes calcium (500 mg), magnesium (250 mg), zinc (15 mg), selenium (200 mcg), and manganese (10 mg). The presence of these can stop your body from absorbing toxic metals like lead, mercury, and aluminum.

Stronger Chelation Methods

While using the green superfoods, cilantro, and garlic is a form of gentle chelation, stronger methods for this process may be required for people who have high levels of metal toxic burden. A chelating agent is a chemical that removes metals or other chemicals from the body tissues, and you can take it in oral, intravenous, or suppository forms for a period of six weeks to a few months. Chelation requires medical supervision, including regular blood work to check for liver and kidney function. Although chelation as a treatment for depression has not been studied yet, patients report less depression, more alertness, and better memory.

Before trying chelation, please use the gentler detoxification steps outlined in this chapter, which work quite well in most cases. In instances of extreme neurologic symptoms and conditions (such as advanced multiple sclerosis, Parkinson's, Alzheimer's, or other neurological disorders) chelation may be the better option.

A healthy body is a key for a healthy mood. In this chapter, we have talked about what testing is helpful to check out what is going on inside your body and brain. We also discussed the importance of digestion and calming inflammation, and we described how to start to clean out the toxic chemicals that can keep mood low. While this is a lot of information, it is essential to know that there are many factors that can create an unhealthy body as well as poor mood—and that there are steps you can take to reverse the process.

5

Your Daily Regimen: What Supplements Are Right for You?

Pop music is aspirin and the blues are vitamins.

—Peter Tork

Before I get into discussing the rest of the supplements that are helpful in treating depression, I need to share one of my pet peeves regarding the world of supplements and nutritional medicine. Of course I have a strong belief in the use of natural medicines in the forms of supplements: capsules, tablets, liquids, powders, and so on. My concern is that sometimes these supplements become the main focus in treatment, with little time spent on any other treatment methods. Some patients visit a natural or holistic practitioner and leave with $500 to $1,000 in supplements that need to be refilled once a month without ever discussing sleep, diet, spirit, or stress management.

When it comes to chronic disease conditions like depression, I want you to remember that only relying on supplements is not likely to fix the problem. Using Saint-John's-wort in place of Zoloft is not what natural medicine is about. By itself, Saint-John's-wort may work sometimes and may even be less toxic than the pharmaceuticals. But overall, expecting that Saint-John's-wort—or any herb or supplement taken on its own without regard to lifestyle, dietary, or environmental factors—will heal a person is not practical. That approach is not what makes good natural medicine therapy; it's simply substituting an herb for a drug. Please do not allow yourself to be caught in that trap.

Another concern I have is about how natural medicines are researched and depicted. In May 2011, I read a headline that proclaimed: "Vitamin D does not prevent depression." Of course I was interested in reading this. I have used vitamin D for years and have seen excellent results in mood issues, autoimmune diseases, and inflammatory problems. The short story is that a study published in the *British Journal of Psychiatry*, a well-respected journal, gave more than 2,200 females over seventy years old a whopping 500,000 IU shot of vitamin D once a year in the fall or wintertime. What they found out is (1) vitamin D seemed to cause an increased rate of falls and fractures, and (2) vitamin D didn't do anything to prevent mood problems. To me, this study moved so far away from the natural way a person's body works that it was destined to fail. When in the world would you receive 500,000 IU of vitamin D at one time in nature? I doubt the body has any idea how to handle that. Unfortunately, the message the media used was that "people took vitamin D, and it didn't prevent depression." Spreading that skewed message will not help anyone.

If we are to benefit from using natural medicines, we need to study them by first asking the question: How does nature intend this item for our bodies, and can we somehow mimic that with our therapy? Then, we need to study it in a paradigm that also addresses a person's diet, lifestyle, sleep, environmental toxins, and stress. Considering all of these together as part of a synergistic plan helps people every day.

If we simplistically treat with natural medicines in the same way conventional medicine treats with drugs, we will continually yield similar results as the misguided conclusion that vitamin D is not helpful for depression. Medical research is a topic I am passionate about, and it's exasperating to me when the media sways the public against natural remedies due to misinformation, poorly designed studies, and sensationalism.

Supplements are vitamins, herbs, and anything that can be placed in a capsule or made into a powder, tablet, or liquid and used to help the body heal itself. According to *Merriam-Webster's 11th Collegiate Dictionary*, a supplement is "something that completes or makes an addition." Consider the way this book is organized: supplements are discussed only after revealing the basics of diet, lifestyle, sleep, spirit, and stress management. This is because those issues need to be addressed first to allow the body to truly heal the way I know it can. Then we can "complete" or enhance the treatment with the supplement, but supplements themselves are rarely the cure.

Please know I am not trying to dissuade you from using supplements. We talked about a number of them in the blood test section; now we will focus on others that may help you. I have certainly witnessed supplements help patients get better faster, and I have seen them serve as invaluable tools to support patients like you who want to safely and effectively wean themselves off their medications.

OILS FOR GOOD MOOD

Healthy fat and oil intake is key for good mood. The brain is about 70% lipids (fats), so the quality and amounts of the oils we take in will play a strong role in the composition and function of our brain and nervous system.

Fish Oil

As we touched on in chapter 2, fish oil is a needed support for brain function and good mood. It contains the omega-3 fatty acids eicosapentaenoic acid (EPA) and docosahexaenoic acid (DHA). These help the body and brain build new nerve tissue by increasing nerve growth factor (NGF)—a protein needed for the growth and repair of nerve tissue. Fish oil supports the adrenal glands (the little glands on top of the kidneys that help the body during times of stress) and creates a healthier cardiovascular system.

Fish oil creates cell membranes that are flexible, which lowers inflammatory response. Unhealthy saturated fats (from most meats and fried foods) create rigid membranes that keep the immune response red-hot and inflamed. Patients with depression have been shown to have lots of unhealthy arachidonic acid (omega-6 fatty acid) in comparison to omega-3 fatty acid. Taking in fish oil helps lower this ratio.

PET scan studies have helped correlate low levels of good fats in the brain with increased likelihood of depression. For example, low DHA levels in the anterior cingulate and prefrontal cortexes of the brain make these areas overactive. This makes decision making and conflict resolution much harder. Medical science's revered double-blind, placebo-controlled studies have shown that taking EPA and DHA induces longer periods of remission from depression. As such, there are a number of clinical studies supporting the use of fish oil for depression, bipolar disorder, schizophrenia, and even depression associated with Parkinson's disease.

Dosage and Toxicity of Fish Oil

The typical dosage of fish oil is 1 g a day of EPA and about 1.5 g of DHA. Read the EPA and DHA levels on the label of the fish oil you purchase. Read the label closely. If your fish oil product does not break the levels down for you, purchase another one that does. Also of note, you should look for high-quality, pharmaceutical-grade fish oils only, because the lesser-quality versions may have an increased chance of rancidity or contain more toxins or impurities. It's actually quite easy to remove toxins from fish oil through a process called molecular distillation. Any high-quality company uses this process to assure that you are getting clean and pure fish oil.

In my experience, a small percentage of patients experience reflux with fish oil. If this is the case for you, you can try dosing with a meal or on an empty stomach to learn which prevents reflux symptoms. Sometimes capsules are better tolerated, while others think the liquid oil is best for them. Some patients report capsules kept in the refrigerator or freezer reduce reflux and fishy breath. If none of these suggestions eliminate reflux, try enteric-coated capsules. Although these capsules are typically more expensive and can be difficult to swallow, they are effective.

Fish oil is extremely safe to take. However, there is some concern about taking fish oil with anticlotting drugs. If you are on anticlotting medications and want to start fish oil, talk to your doctor about slowly adding small amounts of fish oil and checking your clotting factors regularly (using thrombin time, prothrombin time, and INR blood tests) until you are up to the full dose. Your doctor can adjust your medication as needed. If you and your doctor decide to use both treatments together, it's important to stay consistent with your daily fish oil intake and medication intake once you move up to the full dose.

Food Sources of Fish Oil

Not surprisingly, fish is by far the number one source for fish oil. One small study supports the notion that portions of salmon or tuna twice weekly may be as effective as fish oil supplementation to raise omega-3 fatty acid levels. Other studies show that food intake may also allow for better omega-3 absorption. Small fish such as anchovies, herring, and sardines are potent omega-3 sources. Larger fish such as tuna, shark, swordfish, mackerel, and salmon may be contaminated with mercury and harmful pesticides, so use caution to learn origination when choosing caught fish. Chicken, eggs, and beef can also be sources of omega-3 fatty acids if the animals ate green plants and not just grains. Free-range, grass-fed animals are recommended.

Vegan Oils

Many patients ask me about using a vegetable oil, for they are practicing vegans and prefer not to take in any animal products. Vegan fatty acids have not been well studied in mood disorder. In some cases, people with depression are not good at converting plant fatty acid to EPA, which suggests that fish oil may be a better choice.

If you will be using vegan oils, read the label to check for 4 g of alpha-linolenic acid (ALA). This level should ensure that the body forms significant amounts of EPA and DHA. However, it's also important for vegetarians to ensure that their intake of linoleic acid (LA) is not too high compared with ALA, as this imbalance interferes with the body's ALA to EPA and DHA conversion process. An LA-to-ALA ratio of 4:1 or slightly lower is optimum. The best vegan sources of omega-3 fatty acids are flaxseed, grape seed oil, walnuts, and tofu.

Gamma Linolenic Acid

Related to healthy oils, gamma-linolenic acid (GLA) is a fat that can help produce prostaglandin E1 (PGE1), an immune system molecule that helps with mood. Many people who are depressed have a deficiency of delta-6 desaturase, the enzyme that converts LA to PGE1 (see diagram). Chronic stress, diabetes, obesity, age, excess insulin, coffee, trans fatty acids (hydrogenated oils), and alcohol also inhibit activity of this enzyme. For people with this enzyme deficiency, taking supplemental GLA can be helpful. The nutrients vitamin B_6, zinc, and magnesium also aid in this reaction.

GLA-PGE1 Pathway

Vegetable fats → Linoleic Acid (LA) + delta-6 desaturase →
Gamma-Linoleic Acid (GLA)→DGLA → PGE1
(Happy Mood)

People of certain ethnicities tend to have deficiencies of the delta-6 desaturase enzyme needed to make PGE1. This deficiency is especially common in people whose ancestry is 25 percent or higher Celtic, Irish, Scottish, Welsh, Scandinavian, or Native American— which are also groups known to have higher rates of alcoholism.

Have you ever wondered why alcoholics like to drink? Well, it might be because it helps their mood: alcohol can temporarily stimulate production of PGE1 and help lift mood, until PGE1 levels fall again and depression returns. For alcoholic individuals, this results in a cycle of looking to alcohol to feel better. Even individuals without delta-6 desaturase enzyme deficiency can deplete DGLA with repeated drinking by preventing timely replenishment from LA. The people also find the need for more and more alcohol to transiently increase PGE1 to lift mood. Fortunately, you can take in GLA in the form of evening primrose or borage oil, and it's easily converted to PGE1. For alcoholics, these oils can help eliminate both the depression and the need to drink for relief.

Dosage and Toxicity of GLA

Good sources of GLA include evening primrose oil and borage oil. Recommended GLA dosage ranges from 1,000 mg to 2,500 mg once a day. In most preparations, evening primrose oil is usually dosed between 4,000 and 8,000 mg a day, and daily borage oil doses would be about 10,000 mg to achieve recommended levels of GLA. These dosages amount to less than 3,000 mg of GLA per day, which is the upper limit. Doses higher than 3,000 mg of GLA per day should be avoided due to possible exaggerated arachidonic acid levels, which may exacerbate inflammatory reactions. Premenstrual symptoms such as breast tenderness, feelings of depression, irritability, swelling, and bloating may also be indications for GLA supplementation.

Pregnant patients and those with epileptic history or prostate cancer risk should not use GLA supplementation.

Food Sources of GLA

Black currants are a source of GLA.

VITAMINS FOR BODY AND MIND

The following vitamins are discussed individually regarding their potential mood benefits. Some may be included in your multiple vitamin, while some may be best taken as supplements. Follow the dosages given here to ensure for the best benefit.

Be careful to not overdose on vitamins, especially any fat-soluble vitamins (including vitamin A, vitamin D, vitamin E, and vitamin K). Although quite safe at suggested doses, fat-soluble vitamins can collect in your system and become toxic when the levels are too high.

Vitamin D

Vitamin D is a critical hormone and co-factor for many body processes that regulate healthy immune function, cardiovascular function, and nervous system health. Please see chapter 4 where I discuss how to test and dose this vitamin for best mood results.

Selenium

Selenium is important as an antioxidant and for the thyroid. It's the cofactor for glutathione peroxidase, an enzyme that is important to help your body produce its most powerful antioxidant, glutathione. Regarding the thyroid, selenium helps convert the thyroid hormone T4 (thyroxine) to its active form of T3 (triiodothyronine), which helps with clear thinking, mood, fat burning, and even cholesterol levels. Research reports that low selenium is associated with increased depression, anxiety, confusion, and hostility. Conversely, high dietary or supplementary selenium has been shown to improve mood. Even more, when alcoholism and depression occur together with low selenium status, this deadly combination will increase the risk of suicide.

Given the tendency for low selenium status in alcoholics and the relationship between selenium levels and mood disorder, selenium supplementation is recommended for people struggling with depression, alcohol abuse or dependence, or both.

Dosage and Toxicity of Selenium

I use selenium for patients with thyroid issues and alcohol addiction. Common dosages range from 200 to 400 mcg. (Please note this is not milligrams, but micrograms, which is 1/1000th of a milligram. So we are talking about very small amounts.) Overall, selenium is quite safe when taken in prescribed doses.

Food Sources of Selenium

Nuts are a great source of this mineral, especially Brazil nuts. Other sources are fish (especially orange roughy and tuna) and whole wheat flour.

Chromium

As we discussed in chapter 4, poor blood sugar control (low blood sugar, fluctuating blood sugars, or high blood sugar and diabetes) contributes to mood problems and has been correlated with moderate to severe depression. The essential trace element chromium is a component of your body's glucose tolerance factor, a complex molecule your body uses to help balance blood sugar. Chromium also helps by activating serotonin and increasing your body's ability to recognize insulin (known as insulin sensitivity—a big problem for diabetic patients).

Chromium picolinate is one of the few forms of chromium. One study of chromium picolinate looked at fifteen patients with atypical types of major depressive disorder, a type of depression that constitutes more than 20 percent of all cases of depression. This type of depression can be confusing to diagnose, and even more confusing to treat effectively. Atypical depression patients experience symptoms that are different from the majority of depressed patients, including a brightened mood in response to positive events and a depressed overreaction to perceived criticism or rejection. Also, they may have feelings of physical heaviness (lead legs) and struggle with weight gain, increased appetite and carbohydrate cravings, and too much sleep. Please see the following box for a summary of these symptoms.

WHO	ATYPICAL DEPRESSION SYMPTOMS
Everyone	Very sensitive to rejection, carbohydrate craving
Adults	Body symptoms: lead legs, headache, fatigue, digestive disorders
Seniors	Confusion, lowered thinking ability, overall low function
Children	Irritability, decline in school, lowered social interest

In this study, ten patients with atypical depression were started on a low dose of 400 mcg to 600 mcg a day. The other five patients took a placebo. An impressive 70 percent of the patients on the chromium responded positively to the treatment where none of the placebo patients had a positive response. The chromium picolinate was well tolerated with no noticeable side effects.

A second study in 2003 from Duke University looked at 113 patients with atypical depression for eight weeks who received either 600 mcg of chromium or a placebo. Unlike the earlier smaller study, there was no difference in mood itself, but issues with appetite, eating, carbohydrate craving, and mood variation all improved. The patients experiencing carbohydrate cravings had the best results of all. These two studies leave us unsure whether chromium by itself can create healing for depression, but it is pretty clear to me that it can address the blood sugar and appetite aspects of mood, which can play a strong role in moving you toward your healing goals. If you have carbohydrate cravings or have been diagnosed with atypical depression, chromium is certainly worth trying as part of your overall naturopathic protocol.

Dosage and Toxicity of Chromium

Chromium has no known side effects at the standard dosage of 400 to 600 mcg per day. It may be dosed higher under supervision of your doctor.

Food Sources of Chromium

Onions, romaine lettuce, and tomatoes are top chromium sources. Brewer's yeast, liver (I am sure everyone reading this loves liver), bran cereal, and oysters are also good sources. If you do purchase liver, choose meat that comes from naturally raised animals to avoid toxins that the liver can store.

Vitamins B_3 and B_6

B vitamins play an important role in your brain's ability to produce neurotransmitters and your body's ability to make good feeling prostaglandins like PGE1 (see the GLA section in this chapter).

Vitamin B_3

Known for its effectiveness as a treatment in anxiety conditions, vitamin B_3 (niacinamide) is known to inhibit the enzyme tryptophan pyrrolase, thereby helping the body produce serotonin for your brain. Vitamin B_3 is also responsible for helping convert tryptophan to 5-hydroxytryptophan. So it helps in at least two ways to make the mood-elevating neurotransmitter serotonin.

Vitamin B_6

Vitamin B_6 (pyridoxine) is a main cofactor in converting L-tryptophan to serotonin, so vitamin B_6 deficiency contributes to low mood and depression. I should mention that one study found little improvement using solely supplementation with vitamin B_6 versus placebo. This suggests that B_6 deficiency is not a likely sole cause.

Dosages and Toxicity of B_3 and B_6 Vitamins

B vitamins are water soluble and generally safe. Taking 100 mg of B_3 several times daily with meals may also enhance the effectiveness of tryptophan doses. Dosage of vitamin B_6 is usually 20 mg twice a day. Prolonged high doses (200 mg or more a day) of vitamin B_6 may cause a tingling feeling in the hands and feet along with fatigue. Do not use more than 100 mg per day of B_6 to be safe.

Food Sources of B_3 and B_6 Vitamins

Excellent sources of vitamin B_3 include tuna and mushrooms. Sources of vitamin B_6 include bell peppers, bananas, turkey, salmon, spinach, turnip greens, garlic, kale, brussels sprouts, and cod.

Zinc

Known as a mineral cofactor, zinc is responsible for many aspects of our health, including wound healing as well as immune and nervous system balance. For people who are depressed, the lower their zinc levels, the higher their depression severity. Like folic acid, lower serum zinc might help drugs that are not working be more effective (see chapter 7 for more information). One study suggests that zinc may protect brain cells by blocking the toxic effect of glutamate.

Dosage and Toxicity of Zinc

Optimal zinc dosage is 15 to 30 mg a day. It should be taken with food due to the possibility of gastric upset. If you are taking zinc for more than two months, it's best to take 1 to 2 mg of copper every day, for extra zinc can cause the body to lose some copper.

Food Sources of Zinc

Known to accompany animal protein, zinc can be found in beef, lamb, turkey, chicken, pork, crabmeat, lobster, clams, and salmon. The highest vegetable source is pumpkin seeds.

Magnesium

Magnesium is one of my all-time-favorite nutrients. Though known to be beneficial to the heart, relaxing to the muscles, and calming to the mind, it's rarely thought about for low mood and depression.

However, I have relied on magnesium for my own mood balance, and I consider it a strong ally for many of my patients.

Although generally unrecognized, magnesium deficiency has been reported in up to 80 percent of depressed patients, with suicidal patients showing low levels in spinal fluid. Magnesium is an essential trace mineral that is often quite low in the standard American diet, as we strip away many nutrients from our food when they are processed. For example, only 16 percent of the original magnesium remains in refined flour, and magnesium has been removed from most drinking water supplies. Furthermore, carbohydrate consumption and mineral flushing can contribute to low magnesium levels in the body. Simple carbohydrates like white flour bread, cake, and cookies are dangerous; not only do they lack good quality nutrients, but they also cause blood sugar dysregulation and deplete minerals from the body.

One recent study of 5,708 Norwegian people aged forty-six to seventy-four years found that the lower the magnesium intake, the worse the mood. Four published case studies showed that patients recovered from major depression in less than seven days when they took 125 to 300 mg of magnesium (in the forms of glycinate or taurinate) with each meal and at bedtime.

Magnesium deficiency can also contribute to inflammation. Nervous tissue becomes damaged easier, thus increasing inflammation and compounding the chance of depression. Other studies have shown that low magnesium causes inflammation and raises CRP (see chapter 4).

Dosage and Toxicity of Magnesium

Typical dosages of magnesium range from 300 to 700 mg a day. Magnesium is quite safe. However, supplementation is not recommended for patients who have kidney problems. Sometimes magnesium causes a looser stool, and non-chelated forms such as magnesium sulfate (as found in Epsom salts), oxide, hydroxide, or chloride typically encourage diarrhea sooner than the chelated malate, citrate, or glycinate forms. For patients with mood issues, I typically recommend the magnesium glycinate form over other types.

Food Sources of Magnesium

You can find magnesium in mineral water. In fact, many experts believe it's the French's affinity for mineral water that keeps their hearts healthy despite their tendency to eat richer foods. Also, Swiss chard, summer squash, blackstrap molasses, spinach, mustard greens, halibut, turnip greens, and seeds (pumpkin, sunflower, and flax) are good sources.

AMINO ACIDS FOR THE BRAIN

Amino acids play a special role in helping mood. While most vitamins and minerals act as helpers in the production of neurotransmitters, amino acids are the building blocks of neurotransmitters, and they play a central role in helping change your mood for the better.

Tryptophan and 5-Hydroxytryptophan

Tryptophan is an amino acid precursor to serotonin and may be one of the most popular amino acids for mood and sleep. It is a potent antioxidant. Research shows that tryptophan is significantly lower in depressed subjects than in normal controls. And, expectedly, it has been found that depleted levels of 5–hydroxytryptophan (5-HTP), which is made from tryptophan, may increase the risk of a suicide attempt in depressed patients.

Tryptophan → 5-HTP → Serotonin → Better Mood

The desired therapeutic effect of antidepressant drugs known as serotonin reuptake inhibitors (SSRIs) is to increase levels of serotonin by slowing the brain from breaking it down. Supplementing with tryptophan or 5-HTP gives the body more building blocks to make more serotonin. Many natural medicine practitioners believe using tryptophan or 5-HTP is a better method of achieving the same goal as antidepressant drugs, for it allows the body more control over this process and may avoid side effects common in SSRIs.

When supporting serotonin, it's vital to consider the role and health of the digestive tract. As we discussed in chapter 4, digestive dysfunction, abnormal serotonin levels, and psychiatric illness are linked. Effectively treating digestive dysfunction and combining foods to optimize tryptophan uptake may rebalance tryptophan and serotonin levels, thus working to alleviate depressive illness. The naturopathic notion of "treating the gut" may be of important use in treating depression by increasing overall serotonin levels.

Despite anecdotal evidence, relatively few studies have used tryptophan and 5-HTP. With drug popularity, much of the research on these has been discontinued. One recent meta-analysis looking at 108 studies of tryptophan and 5-HTP found only two studies, with a total of sixty-four patients, that met sufficient quality criteria. These studies did suggest 5-HTP and L-tryptophan are better than placebos at alleviating depression. This is a better score than antidepressants get, for antidepressants don't work as well as placebos. Still, more quality research on a large number of individuals is very welcome.

Dosage and Toxicity of Tryptophan and 5-HTP

If patients want to use natural remedies and avoid medication, I highly recommend supplementing a high-quality-grade tryptophan or 5-HTP. If considering one or the other, I recommend starting with 5-HTP, which has been shown to be more effective at crossing the blood-brain barrier to get into the brain. Also, if 5-HTP is taken orally, the process of converting to serotonin absorbs 70 percent of 5-HTP versus only about 3 percent of tryptophan, so you can take significantly less.

Doses of 5-HTP can start at 100 mg three times a day and work up to 200 mg three times a day taken on an empty stomach. Because more research is needed to optimize dosing schedule and amounts, it may be best to start with 500 mg per day of tryptophan on an empty stomach and work up to 2 g per day, if needed. If you have trouble staying asleep at night, I often recommend 500 or 1,000 mg of tryptophan taken with some simple carbohydrates, such as a slice of apple, about thirty minutes before bed.

When dosed accordingly, both tryptophan and 5-HTP are quite safe and effective. In 1989, eosinophilia-myalgia syndrome (EMS) caused concern in the United States after about one thousand individuals taking a tryptophan supplement experienced muscle and joint pain, high fever, swelling of the arms and legs, weakness, and shortness of breath. Sadly, there were about thirty deaths. Although the supplement itself was originally blamed and then banned in the United States, contaminants were actually at fault—it had nothing to do with the tryptophan. It had all to do with a company with poor quality control that had no business making supplements. Today, tryptophan is back on the market, and there are no toxicity issues.

Can I Mix 5-HTP or Tryptophan with Drugs?

One concern with tryptophan and 5-HTP is serotonin syndrome—a condition in which multiple SSRI drugs or an SSRI drug combined with a natural therapy may increase serotonin levels. This syndrome can be characterized by agitation, confusion, hallucinations, fast heartbeat, blood pressure changes, feeling hot, coordination issues, hyper reflexes, or gastrointestinal tract symptoms like nausea, vomiting, and diarrhea. Severe cases can cause rapid fluctuation of temperature and blood pressure, mental status changes, and even coma. Serotonin syndrome was reported in a 2005 study of four elderly patients who combined Tramadol and Remeron, two antidepressant drugs. The use of two antidepressant drugs at the same time caused this syndrome, but studies of drugs and tryptophan have been safely conducted.

One eight-week randomized, controlled trial of thirty patients with major depression found that combining 20 mg of Prozac with 2 g of tryptophan daily at the outset of treatment for major depressive disorder appeared to be a safe protocol. It had both a rapid antidepressant effect and a protective effect on slow-wave sleep, with no need for monitoring drug levels.

Although most psychiatrists are afraid to mix natural medicines like tryptophan with conventional medication, this study shows that when done appropriately, the two can be used together successfully and safely. At this time, there are no studies using 5-HTP with an SSRI drug, although in my clinical experience, low doses used with medication are an effective way to avoid raising drug dosage and to help wean patients off from medication (see chapter 7).

With careful dosing of SSRI drugs and tryptophan, supplementation may prove a side effect–free and useful integrative approach to depression. Of course, it's good to let your prescribing physician know if you are working with natural supplements. You can use this book to guide the discussion with your doctor.

Food Sources of Tryptophan and 5-HTP

Tryptophan can be found in all protein foods in small amounts. Relatively high amounts are present in bananas, turkey (which may contribute to the Thanksgiving sleepiness many people experience), red meat, dairy products, nuts, seeds, soy, tuna, and shellfish. There are no food sources of 5-HTP.

Phenylalanine and Tyrosine

Catecholamines refer to the two neurotransmitters epinephrine and norepinephrine (called adrenaline and noradrenaline in England). These are made by your adrenal gland and help you feel awake, alert, and motivated. Major symptoms of depression can arise from catecholamine deficiency.

As tryptophan and 5-HTP are to serotonin production, L-phenylalanine and tyrosine are to the conversion to first dopamine (DA) and then onto epinephrine and norepinephrine (NE).

The Phenylalanine Tyrosine Neurotransmitter Pathway

Phenylalanine → PEA → Tyrosine → Dopamine → Epinephrine and Norepinephrine → Better Mood

CLINICAL CASE: LENORE AND 5-HTP

One very depressed and anxious forty-eight-year-old patient, "Lenore," visited my office after she had tried five different antidepressant drugs over a three-year period. After listening carefully to her story and asking for some testing, I learned her thyroid function was suboptimal; her vitamin D, B_{12}, and iron were low; and her early life experiences produced negative thought patterns that did not allow her have a more positive outlook.

To help, I prescribed for Lenore some essential fatty acids, vitamin D, B_{12}, and iron as well as thyroid support. We worked on her digestion in order to allow better nutrient absorption. I also prescribed 100 mg of 5-HTP twice a day and recommended acupuncture. Meanwhile, she started to work on her negative thought patterns. Her depression lifted in about one month after starting treatment, and she no longer required antidepressant medication. While no medication had seemed to help, an approach working on multiple levels of her health at the same time did the trick.

Phenylalanine is a precursor of brain phenylethylamine (PEA), an amino acid derivative that contributes to overall energy and elevation of mood. Phenylalanine converts to tyrosine, which is in turn converted to dopamine, and subsequently norepinephrine and epinephrine, which stimulates the nervous system. Studies of people who were both phenylalanine and tyrosine depleted paint a picture of those who are less content and more apathetic—does this describe how you feel sometimes?

There are few good depression studies of phenylalanine or tyrosine. In 1975, twenty-three depressed people who didn't respond to drugs were given 50 or 100 mg per day of phenylalanine for fifteen days. By the thirteenth day of treatment, seventeen subjects reported normal mood. A second study in 1986 showed that phenylalanine supplementation elevated mood in thirty-one of forty depressives with 14 g doses of phenylalanine.

Tyrosine may help your body deal with stress and difficult challenges. It significantly helped the symptoms, adverse moods, and performance problems in subjects exposed to 4.5 hours of excess cold and lack of oxygen in a 1989 study. Tyrosine has also been shown to significantly improve mental performance in those with sleep deprivation.

Dosages and Toxicity of Phenylalanine and Tyrosine

If you are overweight, have a strong appetite, experience regular pain (maybe migraines or arthritis), are going through a lot of physical stressors, or have low motivation and apathy, these amino acids may be able to help. I have used tyrosine and glucose tolerance factor (GTF—a supplement that is composed of a natural form of chromium) to help lessen tobacco withdrawal symptoms in patients who were trying to quit smoking.

The L form of phenylalanine may be dosed up to 14 g a day in divided doses. The D form of phenylalanine has been studied in doses of 350 mg per day. As an antidepressant strategy, L-tyrosine may be used in 500 to 1,000 mg doses two or three times a day, with some studies dosing up to 6,000 mg per day in total. Because tyrosine can be stimulating, taking it during the daytime and adding 1,000 to 1,500 mg of L-tryptophan or 50 to 100 mg of 5-HTP at night for sleep may be a good therapeutic combination to help in mild to moderate depression. No known studies have used phenylalanine and tyrosine at the same time.

Taking too much of these amino acids for your body may result in increased blood pressure and emotional jitters, trouble sleeping, or headaches. Phenylketonuria (PKU) is a disorder in which the body fails to turn phenylalanine into tyrosine properly. Those with PKU should not supplement with phenylalanine and should also be wary of artificial sweeteners, which sometimes use it. Have you ever noticed the warnings on diet soda labels?

Tyrosine seems to be generally safe, though doses greater than 9 g have yielded reports of nausea, diarrhea, headache, vomiting, or excessive nervousness. Insomnia can be prevented by avoiding evening supplementation. Tyrosine should not be taken by anyone who is taking monoamine oxidase inhibitors (MAOIs) for depression or by patients with high blood pressure. Tyrosine may also be contraindicated in multiple myeloma, a cancer of bone marrow cells. Patients with Graves' disease or an overactive thyroid should use caution when supplementing with tyrosine because it might boost thyroid hormone levels.

Food Sources of Phenylalanine and Tyrosine

Some of the most concentrated sources of phenylalanine are torula yeast, soybean protein isolate and concentrate, peanut flour, dried spirulina, seaweed, defatted or low-fat soy flour, dried and salted cod, dried or frozen tofu, Parmesan cheese, almond meal, dry roasted soybean nuts, dried watermelon seeds, and fenugreek seeds. Tyrosine is found in fish, soy products, chicken, almonds, avocados, bananas, dairy products, lima beans, and sesame seeds.

Phosphatidylserine

Along with your fatty acids, phosphatidylserine is a major component of your brain nerve cell membranes. It plays a crucial role in the modulation of the stress hormone cortisol, which is known to remain at high levels in depressed people and can destroy areas of the brain when it sustains at high levels. Phosphatidylserine can help reduce your level of cortisol and protect your brain.

In two studies, 800 mg per day of phosphatidylserine followed by exercise lowered cortisol. A study of ten elderly women with major depressive disorders, found that 200 mg daily improved depressive symptoms and memory.

Dosage and Toxicity of Phosphatidylserine

I typically recommend phosphatidylserine for people dealing with great physical stress, poor memory, and high cortisol. You can ask your naturopathic doctor or other holistic practitioner for a saliva cortisol test if you would like to check levels of cortisol in your system. You can take 200 to 800 mg of phosphatidylserine in divided doses per day on an empty stomach. It may be especially useful before stressful situations. One study of 130 patients showed no negative side effects—it was actually a benefit to liver function.

Food Sources of Phosphatidylserine

The sources with the highest levels phosphatidylserine are mackerel, herring, chicken liver, tuna, soft-shelled clams, and white beans. With the exception of the white beans, vegetables overall have insignificant quantities.

S-Adenyosyl-L-Methionine

S-adenyosyl-L-methionine (SAMe) is a naturally occurring molecule involved in the synthesis of various neurotransmitters in the brain. SAMe is not new—its chemistry was described in 1952. It has been in use for decades in Europe and is a prescription medication in Italy, Spain, Germany, and Russia.

Although the antidepressant mechanism of SAMe is not fully clear, with folic acid and B_{12}, it helps create neurotransmitters such as dopamine, serotonin, and norepinephrine—all of which are needed for good mood.

Folate-B_{12}/SAMe Pathway

Folic Acid + Homocysteine + B_{12} (Methylation Reaction) → Methionine → SAMe → Dopamine/Serotonin/Norepinephrine → Good Mood

Without enough SAMe, your body cannot build well-formed fatty myelin sheaths for your nerve cells, which are needed for healthy nerve cell electrical conduction. Low SAMe is associated with high homocysteine levels (see chapter 4), which can increase the brain toxin glutamate. Homocysteine also breaks down the linings of vessel walls, contributing to inflammation and heart disease. All these promote the development of various disorders, including depression, and SAMe can help alleviate them.

SAMe has been found to be safe and effective in the treatment of mild and moderate depression and, according to some accounts, to have a faster onset of action than conventional antidepressants. In a meta-analysis of forty-seven studies, SAMe produced a significant improvement in mood. SAMe treatment was significantly better than placebo. There are a number of studies directly comparing SAMe to tricyclic antidepressants, with eight studies showing equal benefits and dramatically fewer side effects caused by SAMe.

One uncontrolled trial administered doses of 800 to 3,600 mg per day to thirteen depressed patients with Parkinson's disease for a period of ten weeks. Eleven patients completed the study, and ten had at least a 50 percent improvement.

Little research has studied SAMe's treatment of severe depression, so it's unknown whether SAMe would have the same benefits as it's shown for mild to moderate depression. It may be a good first choice for older patients with other health challenges such as cardiovascular disease, Parkinson's disease, or dementia. Three published case reports have shown SAMe to have been used safely and effectively in children.

Dosage and Toxicity of SAMe

Because starting SAMe can cause nausea, I recommend starting with 200 mg twice daily for the first two days. Then increase to 400 mg twice daily on day three, then to 400 mg three times daily on day ten, and finally to the full dose of 400 mg four times daily on day fourteen. Other than possible mild gastric disturbance,

SAMe has no known toxicity. SAMe is expensive, so it may be a little toxic to the wallet.

Food Sources of SAMe

Your body makes SAMe. There are no known food sources.

Melatonin

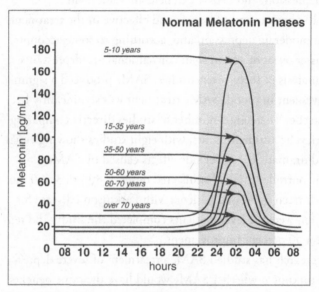

Figure 3: Peak Melatonin at Different Ages

A powerful antioxidant, melatonin is made by a small gland in the middle of your brain called the pineal gland, which secretes this hormone into your system when it gets dark outside. Low melatonin levels have been observed in patients with bulimia, fibromyalgia, breast cancer, and depression. Melatonin causes a surge in serotonin, which helps alleviate symptoms of depressive illness.

Retraining Your Circadian Rhythm

Melatonin's peak release is at night, but it's delayed in people with depression or panic disorder. This is called delayed sleep phase syndrome (DSPS), which makes many depressed people want to stay up most of the night and sleep way too late into the day. If this describes you, you may need to work with melatonin and retraining your circadian rhythm.

People with episodic depression (mild depression that comes and goes) or seasonal affective disorder (SAD) (mild depression that correlates with fall and winter periods of shorter days with less daylight) have lower than normal melatonin levels. Small studies have proven these disorders to be successfully treated with melatonin.

If you are unable to sleep at night and wake up in the morning, then you may want to try the following plan.

Circadian Rhythm Reset Plan

1. Thirty minutes before your eleven p.m. bedtime, take 1 mg melatonin and set your alarm for seven a.m.

2. Wake at seven a.m. and take a supplement of adrenal support. I recommend one that has adrenal gland in it, which can help the body's natural morning rhythm get going. Many adrenal supports also contain vitamin B5 (pantethine) and eleutherococcus, a type of ginseng that is great for supporting adrenal function.

3. Go for a walk outside in bright sunlight. If this is not possible, use a light box with 10,000 lux for thirty minutes.

4. Turn to page 137 and read the list of symptoms treated by the homeopathic remedy staphysagria. If these describe you, take five pellets of a 30C dose once a day for two weeks.

These steps should help reset your circadian rhythm in about four weeks.

Dosage and Toxicity of Melatonin

A common melatonin dosage may be anywhere from 0.5 to 6 mg, thirty minutes before bed. I usually suggest starting with 1 mg doses, and if you feel a bit groggy in the morning, you can lower the dose. If 1 mg does not seem to help you fall asleep, you can increase the dose. Remember, if you have trouble staying asleep, you can work with tryptophan (see chapter 3) or a time-released melatonin, which sustains levels of melatonin throughout the night. Some studies have used very low doses of 0.125 mg in the late afternoon and evening. If you find the later dosing is not working for you, then try the low dose at four p.m. and eight p.m.

Side effects are rare as long as melatonin is taken thirty to forty minutes before a bedtime between ten and eleven thirty p.m. Some literature theorizes that melatonin might make people sadder. Although I have not seen this happen, it's a possibility, so listen to your body. Avoid taking melatonin if you have nighttime asthmatic symptoms.

Food Sources of Melatonin

Oats are known to have a calming effect on the body, and they also contain some melatonin. However, to get the same amount of melatonin that is found in a supplement pill, you would need to eat about twenty bowls of oats. Sweet corn and rice are also sources. Ginger, tomatoes, bananas, and barley contain small amounts of melatonin too.

THE BEST HERBAL CHOICES FOR YOU

The World Health Organization estimates that 80 percent of the world population uses plants medicinally to treat common ailments. About 25 percent of pharmaceuticals have plant origins. Not surprisingly, the botanical pharmacy has a number of strong options for working with depressive illness. Plant medicines are potent allies for patients with depression and are typically less risky than pharmaceuticals.

Saint-John's-Wort (*Hypericum perforatum*)

Honored as the most-studied herb of all time, Saint-John's-wort is a five-petal yellow flowering plant notable for its effectiveness in treating mild to moderate depression. Saint-John's-wort was originally gathered to ward of evil spirits; in fact, its Latin name, *Hypericum perforatum*, means "above a ghost." It is now becoming one of the world's standard antidepressant treatments, according to an article in *CNS Drugs*.

Despite numerous studies, researchers still don't fully understand why Saint-John's-wort effectively treats depression. Initially it was believed to work like the first drugs used for depression, monoamine oxidase inhibitors (MAOIs), which act by slowing the breakdown of neurotransmitters. But later studies suggested it stops the breakdown of the feel-good neurotransmitter acetylcholine, has a serotonin-like activity, or acts like a weak SSRI with fewer side effects. It also gently balances other neurotransmitter levels, including norepinephrine and dopamine, as well as the calming gamma-aminobutyric acid (GABA). It may also encourage production of thyroid hormone. And still other studies show this wonderful herb to have digestive, anti-inflammatory, and nerve-protective properties. Saint-John's-wort produces many helpful changes throughout the body and likely addresses multiple problems that can collectively cause low mood.

While Saint-John's-wort is best known as an antidepressant, it's history has been to help digestion and the nervous system for a variety of issues. The best depression-related use of this herb is for chronic low mood, the kind that keeps you from being happy but not so bad that you can't get out of bed in the morning. The medical term for this is dysthymia.

"Saint-John's-Wort Doesn't Work"

Two well-publicized clinical studies suggest Saint-John's-wort is worthless for depression. When these studies came out, the media gleefully reported that Saint-John's-wort does not work for depression. One of these studies was an eight-week trial that used low doses of 900 mg per day for patients with severe depression. If there was no response to the treatment, doses were increased to 1,200 mg per day. A similar study used 1,800 mg to reach any improvement.

Given that these trials were funded by a company that manu-factures antidepressants, and after a strong history of positive Saint-John's-wort studies, I doubt these publicized studies are valid. My sense is the odds were stacked against the herb by the use of severely depressed patients, the short term of the studies (Saint-John's-wort can take up to twelve weeks to become fully effective), and the small doses. A second eight-week study from 2002 made a similar low dose error. A valuable note in this study is that the comparison drug, sertraline (Zoloft), a drug with a much stronger side-effect profile, was still not any more effective than the under-dosed Saint-John's-wort or the placebo.

The Latest Research for Saint-John's-Wort

The most recent meta-analysis of Saint-John's-wort is a 2008 study from Munich. It reviewed twenty-nine high-quality trials that included a total of 5,489 patients with major depression and compared extracts of Saint-John's-wort with placebo or standard antidepressants including fluoxetine (Prozac), sertraline (Zoloft), imipramine, citalopram (Celexa), paroxetine (Paxil), and amitrip-tyline (Elavil). The studies came from many countries and tested several different Saint-John's-wort extracts. The Saint-John's-wort extracts tested were superior to placebo, and were at least as effec-tive as standard antidepressants. Furthermore, patients given Saint-John's-wort extracts were less likely to drop out of trials due to adverse effects. A very recent study goes on to suggest that side effects of pharmaceutical antidepressants are between ten and thirty-eight times higher than those of Saint-John's-wort.

Dosage and Toxicity of Saint-John's-Wort

Saint-John's-wort dosage usually ranges between 900 mg and 1,800 mg of standardized extract, divided into three doses throughout the day. However, some literature suggests one or two doses a day can be as effective. Common tincture doses range from

20 to 60 drops three times a day of a 1:5 tincture (1:5 stands for the concentration of the whole herb in the liquid). Extracts (which are more concentrated forms) from fresh herb are typically dosed 5 mL two to three times a day. Please check the label of what you are using to check for the type of medicine and concentration.

I typically recommend my patients use a capsule or tablet form standardized for 0.3 percent hypericin. Your label mentions this if it's prepared this way. While hypericin is useful as a standardization, there are many important chemical constituents in this herbal medicine. I enjoy using liquid tincture forms of herbs. If you do too, then look for a liquid tincture that reveals a deep-red color and a nice, potent aroma.

For elderly patients or those with preexisting conductive heart dysfunction, high-dose hypericum extract has been found to be safer with regard to cardiac function than tricyclic antidepressants.

Side effects of Saint-John's-wort are minor, especially when compared to antidepressant medications. Although not reported as a concern with Saint-John's-wort, symptoms of serotonin syndrome (see the discussion in the tryptophan section) should be considered and monitored when combining Saint-John's-wort with antidepressant medication, tryptophan, or 5-HTP.

Saint-John's-Wort Interactions with Other Medications

It has been shown that Saint-John's-wort can either enhance or reduce the circulating levels of other drugs. As a result, it's important to check with your doctor or pharmacist before you start Saint-John's-wort if you are taking medications. There are many medications that may interact that we do not know about, so I recommend against using Saint-John's-wort if you are not sure. Saint-John's-wort is known to impede the effectiveness of the following medications:

Anticoagulants: Phenprocoumon, Warfarin (Coumadin)

Anti-anxiety medications: Xanax (alprazolam)

Antidepressants: Elavil (Amytriptyline)

Antihistamines: Fexofenadine

Birth control pills

Blood pressure medications: Verapamil

Cancer drugs: Irinotecan, Topo II-poison chemotherapy regimens

Cholesterol-lowering medications: Simvastatin

Diabetes drugs: Tolbutamide

Heart medications: Digoxin

HIV medication: Indinavir, Nevirapine, Protease inhibitors

Immune suppressors: Cyclosporine, Tacrolimus

Opiates/addiction drugs: Methadone

Respiratory drugs: Theophylline

Sedatives: Midazolam

On the other hand, new research reports that Saint-John's-wort may even be helpful with certain medications. Plavix is a drug given to many patients who have heart problems to lower clotting effects. About 20 percent of patients who use it do not find any benefit. One study gave 300 mg of Saint-John's-wort three times a day to patients who hadn't been responding to Plavix and found it helped the drug work 36 percent better. This study also noted that patients on medications to lower cholesterol had no negative changes in their cholesterol levels.

Hypericum Plant Spirit

Historically, Saint-John's-wort is particularly useful for patients with feelings of isolation, lack of community, and separation from the rest of the world. It's a wonderful wound healer and gently calms nervous individuals. In my practice, I find that depression dysthymia patients often do the best with this herb. If you can get out of bed and function at a job but are generally low in mood, self-esteem, and zest for life, this may be a good herb for you.

Lavender (*Lavandula angustifolia*)

Used principally as an aromatic essential oil for relaxation, lavender oil in a daily bath can improve mood, reduce aggression, and aid with a more positive outlook. Oral forms of lavender taken with the antidepressant Tofranil (imipramine) were found to be more effective in the treatment of depression than either approach alone, according to a double-blind randomized control trial. This study's double-treatment group took 100 mg of imipramine plus 60 drops of a lavender tincture per day. The findings of this study suggest that taking a moderate amount of lavender may help reduce the amount of tricyclic antidepressants needed to treat depression, leading to fewer side effects. Other studies show taking 80 mg a day of lavender extract is a potent anti-anxiety remedy, comparable to Ativan. Lavender taken orally has also been used traditionally to help spur motivation in people with low mood.

Dosage and Toxicity of Lavender

If patients with depression also have significant anxiety, I recommend they place a few drops of essential oil in the bath with some Epsom salts and take a separate lavender tincture at 30 drops three times a day. Lavender can also be taken as a tea by using 1 or 2 teaspoons of dried lavender flowers per cup of water. This is especially good for a nervous, upset stomach.

Food Sources of Lavender

Essential oils are not to be ingested. Tinctures and teas are effective oral forms of lavender. There are no problems with toxicity when lavender is in the proper form.

Rhodiola (*Rhodiola rosea*)

Adaptogens are plant substances that neutralize low or high levels of hormones and neurotransmitters. Classified as an adaptogen, *Rhodiola rosea* was originally observed in Russian literature as a plant medicine useful to combat physical, biological, and chemical stressors. Looking at a very unique molecule in Rhodiola called rosavin, one mouse study published in *Phytotherapy Research* journal showed both antidepressant and anxiety-reducing effects.

One Armenian clinical trial assessed the efficacy of Rhodiola standardized extract for patients with mild to moderate depression. Over a six-week period, patients taking 340 mg to 680 mg per day found a striking reduction in overall depression over placebo. Out of all the mood parameters tested, the only one not affected for the better was self-esteem (which is an important one). However, when the dose was increased to 1,340 mg per day, self-esteem also improved significantly. Other research used Rhodiola effectively with tricyclic antidepressant medications and demonstrated a significant reduction in medication side effects and a positive influence on psychopathological symptoms in subjects with psychogenic depression.

Dosage and Toxicity of Rhodiola

Dosages of 340 mg to 1,340 mg a day have been used with no toxicities reported. Rhodiola may be standardized for 1 percent of the molecule rosavin. Other studies have used Rhodiola for up to four months without side effects. Longer-term studies of this adaptogen are needed, but what we know so far seems to make rhodiola a great choice if you are feeling depressed, anxious, and burned out.

Saffron (*Crocus sativus*)

Traditionally used in Persia for depression, saffron is known for its vibrant color and flavor and also for being the world's most expensive spice. With a high amount of carotenoids (which give it its burnt orange color) and B vitamins, saffron has been traditionally used as a sedative, an antidepressant, and an anti-inflammatory. It also relaxes the muscles of the digestive tract, reducing spasms and helping digest food, and enhances appetite.

A number of recent studies indicate that the stigma of the plant (the top of the plant where the pollen is), which is technically called the saffron, and petal of *Crocus sativus* plant both have antidepressant effects. In a double-blind, randomized trial, forty depressed outpatients were given either a 15 mg capsule of Crocus petal or 10 mg of fluoxetine (Prozac) in the morning and evening for eight weeks. At the end of trial, the Crocus was found to be as effective as the drug. There were no significant differences between the two treatments in terms of the percentage of responders. Fluoxetine (Prozac) had an 85 percent responder rate, and Crocus petal showed 75 percent. Another study compared Crocus petal to imipramine for six weeks and found a significantly better outcome with the herb.

Dosage and Toxicity of Saffron

While both petal and stigma have antidepressant effects, Crocus petal is less expensive than saffron. No toxicity has been reported at 15 mg dosages or when ingested in culinary amounts. One study showed that when very high levels of saffron were injected directly into rats' abdomens, the animals showed reductions in red blood cells as well as changed liver and kidney function. It should be noted that these are much higher doses than used clinically, and belly injection doses of any otherwise safe food could cause problems in the body. As a precaution, patients with liver and kidney problems may not want to use this herb if other treatment choices are available.

Mucuna Pruriens

Mucuna Pruriens hails from traditional use in Ayurvedic medicine, the traditional medicine of India, and has been used since 1500 BC.

Also known as the velvet bean, this herb has not been studied as an antidepressant in people, but some animal studies suggest possible benefit. It is well-known to contain dopamine (more than any other source). Mucuna has been studied for its effectiveness in helping patients with Parkinson's disease, a condition in which the area of the brain that makes dopamine does not function. Three studies had patients take an average of 45 g of mucuna seed powder extract (which is equivalent to about 1500 mg L-dopamine) per day and reported significant improvements in symptoms. Another study suggested mucuna might have fewer side effects than standard Parkinson's medication.

My interest in mentioning this herb is for those of you who may be using dopamine-boosting medications like bupropion (Wellbutrin, Zyban) or aripiprazole (Abilify) successfully. Patients who have found these to help with motivation, self-esteem, and general good mood may be able to use low doses of this herb to successfully wean off medication while still keeping their better mood intact.

Dosage and Toxicity of Mucuna

For support with medication, I recommend starting with 200 mg of Mucuna Pruriens extract per day and moving up to 200 mg twice a day after two weeks (which supplies about 120 to 240 mg of L-dopamine). This is a relatively low dose. Mucuna may cause some bloating and nausea in some people and can interfere with anticoagulant drugs. It may boost testosterone and could aggravate polycystic ovarian syndrome (PCOS) in women. There have been reported cases of severe vomiting, heart palpitations, difficulty in falling asleep, delusions, and confusion. To be safe, I recommend working with a knowledgeable practitioner if you would like to try this herb.

Sage (*Salvia officinalis*)

The word *sage* comes from the Latin word *salvare*, which means "to heal." Although short on formal clinical studies, sage has long been used for purification, protection, and longevity. The plant has been used in healing ceremonies by the Mazatec Indians of Oaxaca for centuries, and Native American rituals use the smoke from dried sage to eliminate negative spirits. In smudging ceremonies, which clear the psychic space of an area, bundled sage is burned so the smoke can fill the space. It's believed that when inhaled, sage can bring old, buried issues into conscious awareness, allowing the person to release them and move on in life. Anecdotally, sage is also used internally in small doses. It's believed that just a nibble helps people break through repetitive patterns that keep them depressed. Sage tea also acts as a digestive stimulant and has been known to raise the spirits of those with depression.

Dosage and Toxicity of Sage

My experience has been with using sage in smudging ceremonies with patients. Used as an anti-fever treatment, garden sage tea may be a reasonable choice to try. Sip one hot cup every four hours. Sage in these forms has no known toxicity.

Salvia Plant Spirit

Much of what we know about plant medicine we owe to the brilliant Native American healing tradition. The following is a passage from *Sacred Sage: How It Heals* by Silver Wolf Walks Alone, and I believe it truly captures the essence of the Native American use of sage:

> I truly felt the power of the sage plant one time when I was very depressed and could not shake it off. I was wearing depression like an animal wears its fur. I decided to "smoke" it off. I went into a small room in my home and made a comfortable place to sit and lay down. I closed the door to the rest of the house and cracked the window. In my shell, I placed a large ball of sage leaves and lit them. The sage smoldered for at least a half hour. The room was heavily smoked, and I was resting peacefully. I had let my intentions be known through a prayer: I was ready to release this depression and was humbly asking for the help for the sage plant's Spirits and the Creator. When I noticed all the sage was burnt and the smoke was disappearing, I was indeed feeling better. With true desire and clear intention, and focus of action, healing can always occur.

CLINICAL CASE: MARY'S SMUDGING CEREMONY

When Mary came to my office for the first time, during the economic crisis of 2008, she was completely distraught. She worked for a major bank that was in trouble, and she shared with me that she had just been fired by a manager who also happened to be her best friend. This was following a month-long period in which she had lost her mother to Parkinson's disease. Mary had already battled depression and dysthymia for many years. What was going on was now too much.

Mary had never considered suicide, but she said she could see why people no longer have hope when everything around them seems to have been destroyed. For her first visit, Mary and I discussed everything she was feeling and talked about getting some blood tests as well as about taking some tyrosine and fish oil. We also discussed the idea of this time of her life as a place to bring in things that were missing: she always wanted to work with children, she wanted to travel, and she wanted to find someone she loved to travel with as well. We placed this on her to-do list. Mary had never had acupuncture, so we decided to try it at this first visit. During the acupuncture, I burned some sage and explained to her the Native American smudging ritual and its cleansing and healing effects.

Mary left the office feeling much less distraught. She had a plan for the future as opposed to simply dwelling on the past and anxious present. I told Mary we still had work to do.

Obviously, this is not a controlled study. It's possible the sage and acupuncture helped Mary to feel better simply because she was listened to and cared for. Or it's possible that the sage was transformative and allowed her to see the blessings and hope in her life among the destruction.

ENERGETIC HELP WITH HOMEOPATHY

Homeopathy is an energetic system of medicine founded by the American medical doctor Samuel Hahnemann, who is the namesake of Hahnemann University Hospital, part of Drexel University

College of Medicine. Homeopathy is commonly used in Western Europe, India, and Latin America. While slow to adopt natural medicines, North America has begun to see a rapid increase in homeopathy usage. A number of observational studies have shown positive results for homeopathy in conditions such as chronic illness, diabetic neuropathy, and cancer. Patients rightly perceive homeopathy as a lower-risk therapy than conventional treatments and report higher satisfaction rates. Despite this widespread use, relatively scant research has been performed to study the use of homeopathy for depression.

Probably one of the strongest studies to date for homeopathic treatment of depression is a 1997 study out of Duke University, which studied selected remedies on an outpatient basis to treat twelve adults who had major depression, social phobia, or panic disorder. The patients either requested homeopathic treatment or received it on a physician's recommendation after partial or poor response to conventional therapies. Patients were prescribed individual homeopathic prescriptions based on their particular symptoms and personalities for periods of time ranging from seven to eighty weeks. Overall positive response rates were between 50 percent and 58 percent. Although there was some confusion regarding some of the results, and there was no control used to judge the treatments against, the authors concluded, "Homeopathy may be useful in the treatment of affective and anxiety disorders in patients with mildly to severely symptomatic conditions." This study was a good first step, but more is needed.

According to Dr. Dana Ullman, there are "literally hundreds" of possible remedies for depression. Although not exhaustive, the following is a list of common homeopathic remedies for depression, each followed by a condensed list of symptoms the remedy treats. Try looking at these lists to see which best describes you. You may not experience every symptom in a description, but if the overall description sounds like you, then you can give that particular remedy a try.

Arsenicum album

- Demanding personality
- Insecurity and anxiety
- Depression with impossibly high expectations of yourself and others
- A strong sense of dependency

Aurum metallicum

- Impatience and tendency to interrupt others, walk and talk at a fast pace, anger easily, and be curt or rude
- Depression when you perform poorly or when you feel you do not live up to your expectations and sense of ability
- Serious outlook and believe yourself worthless
- Despair about life
- Discouragement
- Humiliation and anger, which lead to feelings of emptiness and worthlessness
- Emotional sensitivity
- Sensitivity to noise and light
- Increase in physical and emotional symptoms at night
- Nighttime head pain and high blood pressure
- Nightmares or insomnia

In extreme cases, people who are considering suicide or have attempted it may find relief with Aurum. According to Dr. William Mitchell, Aurum is a good choice for patients with depression and suicidal tendency, for which a 200X or 200C potency can make them feel like the light has been turned on. X and C refer to the strength of the homeopathic preparation. Mitchell found it effective to dose Aurum one time each day until symptoms clear. If you have suicidal thoughts, or have had them recently, please first tell a doctor, for he or she can help you. Then, look for Aurum.

Calcarea carbonica

- Overall personality is mild and gentle
- Dependable and industrious person who becomes overwhelmed from too much worry, work, or physical illness
- Frequent crying
- Anxiety, fatigue, confusion, discouragement, self-pity, and mood swings
- Dread of disaster
- Childlike desire to be consoled and gain sympathy, especially when given by a mother-like figure
- Aversion to conflict
- Difficulty making decisions
- Sluggishness after exertion
- Increased depression before or during menstruation
- Elevation of symptoms in stuffy rooms
- Craving for rich, fatty foods and eggs
- Perspiration while eating

Causticum

- Continual grief
- Frequent crying
- Mental dullness and forgetfulness
- Severe discouragement
- Sense of injustice in the world and sympathy toward those who are wronged

Cimicifuga

- Energy and talkativeness when feeling well but gloominess when depressed

- Exaggerated fears of things like going insane, being attacked, or suffering disaster
- Painful menstruation
- Headaches that involve the neck

Ignatia amara

- Sensitive person who has suffered grief, loss of loved ones, and/or disappointment and tries to keep the hurt inside
- Defensiveness to avoid showing hurt
- Inappropriate laughing or crying
- Plum pit qi (the Chinese medicine term for a lump in the throat) and heaviness in the chest
- Frequent sighing or yawning
- Insomnia or excessive sleeping
- Headaches and cramps in the abdomen and back

One study with ignatia for patients with fibromyalgia showed a trend toward less depression as well as less tender points and pain, and better quality of life and health.

Kali phosphoricum

- Increased depression after stressors like excess work, illness, emotional strain, or excitement
- Exhaustion
- Nervousness and jumpiness
- Low concentration that leads to lack of confidence
- Headaches from mental effort
- Easy perspiration
- Sensitivity to cold
- Anemia
- Regular insomnia and indigestion

Natrum carbonicum

- Depression after an injury, disappointment, or illness
- Personality is mild, gentle, and selfless—making an effort to be cheerful and helpful
- Conflict aversion
- Privacy with feelings of depression
- Preference for sad music when lonely, leading to feelings of isolation
- Emotional and physical sensitivity to sun, weather changes, and many foods, especially milk

Natrum muriaticum

- Betrayal by trusted people
- Depression prior to or during menstruation
- Reservation and responsibility
- Privacy with strong inner feelings (anger, grief, romantic attachment, or fear of misfortune)
- Anger when people offer consolation
- Crying—only when alone, with heavy sobbing
- Anxiety
- Tendency to dwell on past grievances
- Migraines, back pain, and insomnia when depressed
- Craving for salt
- Elevation of symptoms during hot weather, fatigue with sun exposure
- Perceived or actual lack of bonding or nurturing from mother or father

Natrum Sulphuricum

- Depression or mood change after head injury

- May have pain in the back of the head
- Worse with wet, damp, and humid conditions
- Better with dryness
- Sensitive to criticism

Phosphoricum Acidum

- Emotional and physical fatigue
- Graying or loss of hair after severe depression or grief
- Loss of interest in activities or items previously favored
- Increased fatigue and depression after exercise
- Emotional numbness or indifference
- Emptiness
- Lack of concentration
- Perceived lack of intelligence
- Loss of motivation at work, lack of interest in business matters
- Tendency to dwell on disappointment
- Oversensitivity to lights, sounds, and odors
- Physical weakness in the morning
- Mood drops when exposed to cold outdoors or drafts

Pulsatilla

- Crying, desire for consolation and hugs
- Childlike softness and sensitivity
- Whininess, jealousy, or moodiness
- Mood elevation with crying, gentle exercise, or fresh air
- Increased anxiety in hot or stuffy environments
- If female, worse depression during hormonal changes (such as puberty, menstruation, or menopause)

Sepia

- Great fatigue from daily life
- Preference for being left alone, not consoled
- Indifference to family members
- Menstrual problems
- Sense of organ prolapse (the falling or slipping down of an organ, such as the uterus)
- Very slow digestion
- Elevated mood after vigorous exercise or crying

Staphysagria

- Depression, shame, resentment, or humiliation because of an insult or loss of pride
- Suppressed emotions
- Depression after a bout of anger
- Attachment to dignity when feeling beaten down
- Anger fits under pressure
- Emotional sensitivity
- Trembling associated with strong emotions
- Strong sexual desires and frequent masturbation
- Self-pity
- Sensitive and difficulty standing up for self
- Upset circadian rhythm
- Pains manifesting as toothaches, headaches, stomach aches, or bladder infections

Dosage of Homeopathics

As is true for many forms of natural medicines, different sources recommend various methods of dosing. I usually recommend patients take one dose per day of a higher potency such as 200C, and give two weeks for a response. If you notice an improvement, continue at the same dosage and let the remedy work. If there's no improvement, you can change the dosage or remedy. With homeopathy, listen to your body—and try to assess if you are feeling better. If you think some of your symptoms have gotten worse. it may be best to try another remedy. If you are not sure how to best approach it yourself, consult your homeopath or a practitioner who is knowledgeable of homeopathic medications.

A COLD SPLASH: WATER THERAPY

Hydrotherapy may be defined as the use of water, in any of its forms, for the maintenance of health or the treatment of disease. It has been employed since ancient times as a way to balance the body and mind. According to Hippocrates, water therapy "allays lassitude."

Have you ever taken a cold swim? How does it make you feel? After you get over the initial shock of the cold, it's usually very invigorating. This is because when you go to a cold temperature quickly, your blood moves from the surface of your body to the core, and this helps bathe your brain and organs in fresh blood while also cleaning out your system.

Throughout evolution, primates have endured physiological stressors like swimming through a cold river or hunting in very hot weather. Naturopathic hydrotherapies are designed to take advantage of the natural body reaction to these stressors. It has been theorized that brief changes in body temperature are important for proper brain function. As I have seen it help other people with low mood, hydrotherapy may help you return some of the good old-fashioned physical "stressors" that are missing in modern life.

One group of researchers in Virginia suggests that hydrotherapy may be useful to treat cancer and chronic fatigue as well as depression. Cold exposure therapies may actually be the best choice for depressed patients. The simultaneous firing of all skin-based cold receptors—thought to be three to ten times denser than warm receptors—from jumping into the cold may result in a positive therapeutic effect. It has also been shown that lowering brain temperature protects neurons and decreases inflammation. In addition, exposure to cold has been shown to activate the sympathetic nervous system, increase the blood level as well as brain release of norepinephrine, and elevate production of beta-endorphin, a feel-good molecule that gives a sense of well-being.

Cold water exposure may have a mechanism similar to another proven antidepressant treatment: electric shock therapy. Electric shock therapy has long been used to treat drug-resistant forms of depression with a procedure called electroconvulsive therapy (ECT). These effects may well help depressed patients, especially those who do well with increased release of norepinephrine as with duloxetine (Cymbalta) or other serotonin norepinephrine reuptake inhibitors (SNRIs).

Dosage and Toxicity of Hydrotherapy

I recommend patients with depression use a brief whole-body exposure to cold water in the form of a cold shower. Start the shower at a comfortable warm temperature and slowly cool the water over a five-minute period down to 68 degrees Fahrenheit, and stay at that temperature for two to three minutes. You can use a thermometer to check the temperature as you go. This can be performed once or twice a day for a duration of a couple weeks to several months.

Although mild cold stress seems to help the brain work better, animal research has shown that extreme cold may actually worsen mood. To avoid this, follow the directions I've detailed here.

CLINICAL CASE: LEN'S RETURN TO THE WATER

Len is a thirty-seven-year-old film music production technician who came to my office with a diagnosis of irritable bowel syndrome and anxiety. His digestive system had started going awry about a year earlier, and he had to run to the bathroom because of gas and diarrhea a few times a day. After a colonoscopy and a few visits, Len's gastroenterologist recommended he start Imodium to stop the diarrhea and antidepressants to suppress both his anxiety and the nervous function of the intestines.

I asked Len what had been going on in his life when this started. He had recently taken a "real job" in music production, for his own music writing career was not paying the bills and his living situation was too expensive. At that point, two things had changed: he stopped his daily morning swims at the YMCA, and he ate mostly Chinese takeout while slumped over a sound board. As a plan of action, I asked Len to change his takeout food to something more healthy: he found a macrobiotic vegetarian place and a sushi restaurant nearby that delivered. The food change helped about 60 percent after two weeks.

At that point, I asked Len to get back to his exercise routine, which he said he had no time for right then, for the production schedule had him at work early and leaving late. Because exercise was not an option, I asked Len to try contrast hydrotherapy over his abdomen in the shower. I had him first place a few drops of lavender essential oil on the shower floor, so he could smell it as the shower heated. Then he simply turned the water up to a hot (but not scalding) temperature and let it rain on his stomach and intestine area for two minutes. Then he quickly switched it to cold for forty-five seconds. I asked him to repeat this cycle three times. Len wrote to me that "although it seemed time-consuming, it had a wonderful calming effect" on both his mind and his stomach. Within the next week, his bowel symptoms disappeared. Len and I also discussed a plan to move him back into the music writing world and leave his job, which he realized was the catalyst for his original stress.

In this chapter, we've discussed a multitude of supplements and some good old-fashioned water therapy. While all of these are not necessary for all people with depression, my hope is that this information and these patient stories will help you recognize which situations might be most similar to your own so you can pick the best ones to help you feel better.

6

Bringing in the New

The first duty of love is to listen.

—Paul Tillich

My experience working with patients over the years has taught me one thing: no two people are alike, and no two effective treatment plans are alike. As such, it's the priority of a physician like me to first listen and then talk with each patient to figure out together which combination of lifestyle changes, remedies, and therapies may suit the patient the best. It's clear that if you are reading this book, you have a love for yourself . . . and you want to get better. So I encourage you to listen to your heart and spirit as you read the descriptions of these therapies to see which ones speak to you.

In that spirit, this chapter corrals the many different modalities and healing therapies I would like you to consider as you traverse this journey toward healing. New thoughts and experiences will help change your brain and make it new.

Some of these therapies I learned about from my patients. In truth, everything I have learned about medicine and healing, I have learned from my patients—so when a patient tells me something has helped him, I listen very closely in the hope of learning about it myself. This way, I can offer another tool to help future patients. And as a patient, you can look for practitioners like this (see the resources at the end of this book for help with this) and build your own dream team of healers and therapies that you can rely on for support when needed.

The modalities listed in this chapter are very different from each other, in honor of how each of you reading this is very different. The one thing they all have in common is their ability to help depression sufferers, as they continue the journey to understand depression and come to terms with it in a manner that allows them to become closer to the potential of who they really are.

Read through this chapter at your leisure—try to see which modalities speak to you and make sense in your heart. These are the ones you may want to try first.

POSITIVITY WORK

The French have a term, *raison d'être*, which translates as "reason to live." The psychologist Rollo May defined depression as "the inability to construct a future." In cases of depression, there's at some level a lack of perceived reason to live. In the less severe cases, depression sufferers may not enjoy their jobs or relationships and feel blue sometimes. At the most severe level, people truly believe there's no reason to continue on because nothing can get better. If you are reading this book, you are somewhere in that continuum:

Sometimes Feeling Blue → Depressed → No Reason to Live

Analytical Rumination Hypothesis

There's a theory in the psychology world called the analytical rumination hypothesis. The basic idea here is that your body's depression reaction is a response to help work things out: the body actually makes you move away from perceived danger, withdrawing for protection while it tries to figure out how to change the situation. Two key questions in my mind while working with patients with depression are: What is the depressed body saying to the patients? Can they learn from this?

In his book *Manufacturing Depression*, psychologist Gary Greenberg discusses the idea that "mental illnesses weren't real, but merely ways of pathologizing non-conformity." While mental illness is indeed real, for many people have been depressed, one could argue that depression has helped some create a better life, that depression has been a reaction to living a life not congruent with what society wanted or expected. When I was in my twenties, I was in a rock band. I remember feeling conflicted and quite blue thinking about what my family, society, and friends with "real jobs" thought of me. Did they wonder why I was not a doctor or professional? Though I wasn't clinically depressed, the pressure that came along with bucking societal convention was definitely strong.

Many well-known, amazing contributors to society have battled depression: musicians Sting and John Denver, baseball great Ty Cobb, quarterback Terry Bradshaw, early twentieth-century leaders Winston Churchill and Theodore Roosevelt, and astronaut Buzz Aldrin. Evolutionary biologist Charles Darwin was also depressed. He felt completely held back and debilitated by his mood swings and symptoms. In reference to his low mood, fits of crying, palpitations, and digestive problems, he is quoted as saying: "I shall probably do little more but be content to admire the strides others made in science." An article about the analytical ruminative hypothesis in the *New York Times* explained an interpretation of Darwin's experience: "Instead, the pain (and depression) may actually have accelerated the pace of his research, allowing him to withdraw from the world and concentrate entirely on his work."

The positive impact that Darwin and many, many other people who suffer and have suffered depression have had on our lives is great. Looking at their stories, one could argue that if not for their experience of depression, their lives might not have been so extraordinary. A patient I worked with who was in the midst of a miserable divorce told me, in retrospect, that her pain and depression was the way to get away from the world—"to a place where I could think, plan, and reinvent the person I really wanted to be."

I will tell you that some psychologists and psychiatrists believe the analytical rumination hypothesis is garbage at best, deadly at worst. Deadly, for they are reasonably worried that caregivers who believe depression is only a helpful learning tool may not take it seriously enough to recognize when severely depressed patients need to be treated more urgently. They may be correct, for some people with severe depression might get away from the world to hurt themselves instead of focusing on how to make their situation better. This is where we need to consider all aspects of treatment—natural (foods, lifestyle, herbs, and so on) and conventional (drugs and hospitalization). Safety should be the first priority, and all treatments have their place.

However, I do believe that like its more energetic cousin anxiety, depression is a method for the body to protect itself—and it gives us clues on how to heal in the process. Anxiety increases the stress response (called the sympathetic response) to create an excitable state strong enough to make us get away from danger or perform a feat of survival. Depression also has an increased stress response but instead attempts to get us to crawl back into our shell when danger is sensed.

A patient I recently worked with told me that when his brain was depressed, "it was like a car that would not start. It made me sit parked and think about what was going on in my life until I figured out what to do." This reaction has been described by many of my patients, and can be quite healthy, for it gives a chance to process and make decisions in a space of safety and out of the way of oncoming traffic.

For some depressed patients, and possibly you, these feelings become out of balance, and that space of safety becomes a prison which cannot be easily exited. That means you need more support—which is why this book can be useful. In some cases, these feelings go way too far, to the point where the feelings become a physical danger to the depression sufferer or to someone close to that person. Again, at that point safety may call for medication, psychiatric care, or even a stay in a hospital. Once the danger has passed, then natural means may be the best next step to truly heal the physical, emotional, and spiritual realms.

In my clinical experience, I have found what I call positivity work to be an important approach in changing the patterns and messages in patients' brains in order to move them back toward the left of the depression continuum. Hopefully, they move back so far that they are feeling good. This positivity work includes two aspects: replacing old thoughts and picking one new thing to do.

Positivity Step 1: Replace Old Messages with New Ones

In any form of depression, one restraint that holds people back from being happy lies in the ability of the brain to replay old negative messages over and over. Some of these messages can be

- "I am not worth anything."
- "I am not good at anything."
- "I hate my job."
- "I will not get everything done that I need to get done."
- "I am not lovable."
- "I have no reason to have self-esteem."
- "The world is a bad place."
- "What I did was a mistake."

You get the idea. I am sure you could add your own list to these. In fact, if you feel bold, over the course of a day, I would like you to add to that list. What are you are telling yourself? What messages did someone teach you at a young age, or did you teach yourself? Once you have your list, try to counter these thoughts:

INSTEAD OF SAYING . . .	TRYING SAYING THIS INSTEAD . . .
"I'm not worth anything."	"I am worth a great deal. Everyone is worth a lot, and I have a lot to give."
"I am not good at anything."	"I have a number of things I do well."

INSTEAD OF SAYING...	TRYING SAYING THIS INSTEAD...
"I hate my job."	"My job is not my passion, but it's a blessing that allows me to pay my bills while I figure out what I truly want to do."
"I never feel good in the morning."	"I do get tired in the morning, but as I shower and eat, I always start to feel better. I will be okay today."
"I will not get everything done that I need to get done."	"I will do the best I can today, and that is all I can really ask of myself."
"I am not lovable."	"I am a good person and worthy of other people's love."
"The world is a bad place and people are mean."	"The world is made of lots of people and events, and I cannot take personally what happens sometimes with other people or when challenging things happen. I can learn from these things, though, and make my life even better as I go on."
"I have had this problem a long time. It will never get better."	"Nothing in my brain is hardwired. Feeling better is a process, and it takes time. I am proud of everything I have learned and what I am starting to do."
"I will mess up if I try that."	"There is no such thing as messing up. If it doesn't go right, I will learn something which will help me in the future."
"What I did was a mistake."	"Mistakes are only mistakes when we do not learn from them. What happened is something I can learn from to create an even better life."
"Life isn't fair."	"Life doesn't have anything personal against me—everyone experiences ups and downs."

So, this is probably the part of the book where you are reading this and begin to think, Okay, this guy's in la-la land now. This kind of nonsense can't possibly help me.

Well, if you are only listening to yourself, ruminating on the same negative messages day in and out, then you are right. You will not be able to change those messages and believe new thoughts.

In fact, as time goes on, the same negative messages in your brain will only get more ingrained. There is an old saying that your belief becomes your biology. For every thought we have, brain molecules are being created and others suppressed. You have spent a lot of time not allowing any positive thoughts to mix in, inhibiting the creation of your best mood chemicals. You can break this cycle. It takes practice and habit. It does work, though. I assure you.

So how do you change the negative messages? You bring in other thoughts. Also, you can start bringing in positive people as friends, working with positive counselors and therapists, and continuing to read positive books. I hope this is one of the positive books for you. You may also want to minimize time with the people around you who promote negative messages—sometimes this could even be family and close friends. It's not an easy process, but you are fighting for your health and for your life.

I often read books or listen to lectures together with my patients, or I have them take a book home to read. You can find a list of recommendations at www.drpeterbongiorno.com/positivity. Many of these books bring in Buddhist ideas, some are about relationships, some are lectures on self-esteem while others are about figuring out what makes you happy, and some are just about being positive. They all help reframe various negative messages you are telling yourself. Listen and read them all if you can—the more you bring these ideas into your life, the less room your brain has for negativity.

Reality is truly in your mind—you can create a new reality that honors the positive aspects of your heritage, upbringing, and experiences without grasping the negative messages.

Positivity Step 2: Choose New Experiences

The second part of positivity work is choosing new experiences. These activate the brain's reward system, flooding it with dopamine and norepinephrine. These are the same neurotransmitters that are ignited in early romantic love, a time of exhilaration and obsessive thoughts about a new partner.

Following are some experiences that I have seen particularly useful to spur patients out of depression. One patient even came in one day and said, "Okay, I thought of a new idea: skydiving!" She'd always wanted to try it, and even though it scared her, she realized that not being happy and living a dreary day-to-day life scared her more. So she went skydiving (with a qualified instructor, of course), and soon after, her antidepressant medications were history! Her brain was making those neurotransmitters on its own. No drug can compete with the influx of dopamine a good skydive will elicit.

Listen, you do not have to jump out of an airplane, but do try to be bold and open-minded about trying new things. They can be big experiences like a trip or small ones like buying yourself a new favorite flower.

Ideas for New Experiences:

- Volunteer to help those less fortunate than yourself.
- Purchase an MP3 player and load it with all your favorite uplifting music for exercising.
- Find a good hairstylist and try a new style haircut or color.
- Pick a new set of glasses to wear.
- Schedule time with a loved one to do something fun.
- Sign up for an acting class.
- Start lessons for a musical instrument or buy a self-teaching book.
- Try some new clothes, maybe a style you have not worn before.
- Travel somewhere new. Make sure you take pictures and put them up around you when you get back.
- Try new foods at a restaurant or even cook some at home.
- Buy a new flower for yourself weekly.
- Get a massage.
- Attend a musical event, concert, or play.

- Sign up for an online dating service and meet new people.
- Join a book club.
- Pretend you lost your job and look to see what new opportunities might be around for you.

I promise if you pick up a new book or lecture and start a new activity, your brain will begin switching modes and bring you greater joy in your everyday life. If you are thinking, Well, I would do these things if I wasn't depressed, you are not alone. Try your best to do them, and follow the other recommendations in the book. As we discussed last chapter, sometimes phenylalanine and tyrosine can help the motivation, as can acupuncture. A combination of these things will eventually get you up and moving—just keep doing your best.

PSYCHOTHERAPY

In most cases, psychotherapy is important and useful to treat depression. Emotional processing is useful for low mood, especially when there's a past traumatic or depressing life event. During psychotherapy, you can identify and work through the factors that may be causing depression. This section will briefly survey common forms of psychotherapy.

Psychodynamic therapy is based on the assumption that a person is depressed because of unresolved, generally unconscious conflicts, often stemming from childhood. The goal of this type of therapy is for the patient to understand and cope better with these feelings by talking about the experiences. It is administered over a period ranging from weeks to years.

Interpersonal therapy (IPT) generally focuses on improving communication skills and increasing self-confidence and esteem. It is often used when depression onset stems from the loss of a loved one, life transition (such as becoming a parent or changing careers), feelings of isolation, or relationship conflicts. In a study of 233 women with a history of recurrent depression receiving IPT, half the subjects improved with IPT alone. Interestingly, researchers concluded that frequency of counseling was not a factor—monthly treatments appeared to be as effective as weekly in preventing the recurrence of depressive symptoms. However, they noted that twice-monthly therapy yielded the lowest quitting, suggesting that there may be a best frequency of treatment. If you try IPT, talk about it with your therapist to determine the best visit frequency for you. For the subjects that didn't improve with IPT alone, anti-depressant therapy was recommended. I wonder, if other natural remedies from this book had been used in conjunction with IPT, perhaps the success rate would have been even higher.

Cognitive behavioral therapy (CBT) helps people with depression to identify and change inaccurate perceptions that they may have of themselves and the world around them. The therapist helps patients establish new ways of thinking by directing attention to both the "wrong" and "right" assumptions they make about themselves and others.

Some high-quality studies have suggested that online CBT may hold great value and promise as a therapy. Results based on a data review of 1,746 patients with depression, social phobia, panic disorders, and anxiety showed that about one in two people improved with online CBT alone, which is a pretty good result for a single medical therapy. I was most struck by what Dr. Gavin Andrews, a conventional medicine psychiatry professor from Australia who headed the study, said:

> [T]here was no hint of relapse reported in any study, which is just foreign to my experience. Depression is supposed to be a relapsing and recurring disorder. What on earth is it doing just disappearing after someone does CBT over the Web? This is not what any of us were trained for.

Another study of twenty-six patients hospitalized for severe depression found that mood states improved significantly after one sixty-minute computer-assisted CBT session—let me repeat, that was only one session. This is impressive, for severely depressed patients from an in-patient ward may be the toughest to treat. This study used a commercial DVD-ROM program called Good Days Ahead which costs much less than you would pay for a single session with a psychiatrist or psychologist in most cases. There are also free websites and inexpensive phone applications too. Please see the resources section of this book for CBT resources that you might find helpful.

A note about psychotherapy: The famous medicine intuitive Dr. Caroline Myss has a cautionary saying in her self-esteem lecture series that goes something like this: "Be careful with psychotherapy. It's great at keeping people feeling good in their dysfunction." Remember, when you are working with a psychotherapist, naturopathic physician, acupuncturist, medical doctor, or anyone else, you need to ask them to explain exactly what you are doing together so you understand it. The word *doctor* comes from the Latin *docere*, which means "to teach." So if your doctors are not teaching you—they are not doing the job correctly. Then ask, "How long do you expect to work at this before you start to see changes, and what kinds of changes do you expect to see?"

To be fair to practitioners, sometimes it takes time to see results and the approach will change as you go—and they may need to explain that to you. But if you feel like you are really not making any progress after a reasonable amount of time, you may want to consider working with someone else for a different approach. Sometimes I suggest patients I have been working with start to work with another practitioner if I believe I am not moving them in the right direction within a reasonable time. It's not that I do not believe in my ability, but sometimes the practitioner-patient chemistry is not as healing as it may be with another —and that is okay. We are all different, and we do not completely understand what makes a healing relationship successful. You may need to try a few or more practitioners to find the right healing therapy and chemistry.

CLINICAL CASE: BELLA AND PSYCHOTHERAPY

Bella, a forty-nine-year-old Colombian woman, came to my office with extreme fatigue, increased need to sleep, and depression. After poring over all the possible physical and emotional factors, we learned that her marriage was the greatest source of her stress. Fifteen years prior, she'd had an arranged marriage in Colombia and moved to the United States. Bella explained to me how her husband would continually put her down, verbally abuse her, and create a state in which Bella had no authority. Family and religious obligations prevented divorce from even being an option. Her body was exhausted from the years of caring for her two children, whom she felt she protected from her husband's control.

Once the kids left for college, Bella's depression set in. It had been five years since the youngest child left home, and the depression had progressed through those years. Although we explored the idea of the empty nest syndrome, it became apparent that Bella's depression was centered around her daily feeling of being beaten down by her husband's words. Bella felt trapped with no options.

I referred Bella to a psychologist whose focus was working with women in difficult and violent relationships. Based on her blood tests, we started her on some vitamin D and gave her an anti-inflammatory protocol. We also started adrenal support and melatonin to reset her circadian rhythm, homeopathic Sepia, and acupuncture. Her psychologist had Bella ask her husband to also work with a therapist. Unfortunately, he denied any issues and became angry and insulted when she brought up the subject. With her therapist's suggestion, she then came up with a plan to secure her finances in preparation of letting her kids and husband know that she would separate from him and move in to her own place. Within one month of starting these treatments, Bella's need to sleep decreased, and her energy improved in the afternoon. She was able to successfully and safely extricate herself from the marriage—something she had not thought was a possibility not too long before.

In my opinion, the acupuncture, homeopathy, vitamin D, and anti-inflammatory supported to her body, but they would not have worked without the solid therapy and support work that allowed Bella to create a plan to regain control of her life—in order to get away from the constant sense of danger in which she lived. It is important to remember that, even in cases that seem void of options, patience and consistency will help you learn that there are always options.

YOGA

The term *yoga* is derived from the Sanskrit root *yug*, which means "to join." It signifies union between an individual's soul and the universal soul—what a beautiful idea. I believe it to be a brilliant treatment and very worth your time.

From a spiritual standpoint, yoga is a strong practice that can help modify emotional processing. *Sukha* is the Sanskrit word for happiness and literally translates to "unobstructed peace." Yoga practice is thought to clear blockages within the body, leading to a greater sense of calm and contentment with reality as it is, often with a greater sense of happiness and connectedness to others.

Physically, yoga helps us to focus the mind and achieve relaxation. Like exercise, yoga is an excellent method to deepen the breath and keep blood flowing. Yoga can reduce the stress hormone cortisol, stimulate endorphin production, raise serotonin levels, and increase the relaxation response. Muscle movement pumps lymph tissue and encourages physical cleansing of toxins.

An electroencephalogram (EEG) tests the electrical activity of the brain using electrodes placed on the surface of the head. A small study measured EEG brain waves both before and after two hours of Kriya yoga, a type of yoga designed to remove obstructions to the body and mind. In this class, it was found that alpha and theta waves increased—both signs of happiness. Other studies show that yoga increases brain levels of gamma-aminobutyric acid (GABA), a neurotransmitter that relaxes. GABA is like our brain's natural Xanax. There are a number of types of yoga. From my experience, most forms seem to be helpful—like all other recommendations, listen to your body and choose the one that seems right for you.

CLINICAL CASE: YOGA AND TIM

Tim was a sixty-five-year-old cabinet maker who came to my office feeling dizzy. He had been visiting a psychotherapist for the past six months for increasing feelings of anxiety and depression. Tim had been given antidepressants two years prior after losing two of his closest friends to sickness. Ever since, Tim felt alone.

Tim came in to see me hoping to fix the physical symptom of dizziness as well as a problem gaining weight. After having him checked by a neurologist, we learned Tim seemed to have no organic reason for the dizziness. Although he had never been diagnosed with anorexia, I wondered if this was causing his difficulty gaining weight.

Noticing Tim's blood sugar was a little low, I asked Tim to begin eating small, frequent meals. I also gave him some supplements to support blood sugar (like chromium) and recommended he eat some berries every day. I also asked Tim to sleep a full eight hours every night, which he did. Last, I gave Tim SAMe. He had complained of joint pain, and SAMe is perfect for helping osteoarthritic joint issues as well as mood.

Within two weeks, Tim's dizziness faded away.

Discussing the need for community, I asked Tim if he had ever tried yoga—he had not, but he seemed open to it. In New York City, yoga studios abound—so luckily, there was one close to his apartment. He joined and found a community that embraced him. He decided to go every day.

Within three months, Tim talked to his psychiatrist about weaning off his medication. I started Tim on a little 5-HTP for that process, and within three weeks, he had successfully ended the medication. Tim stopped using the 5-HTP about one month later with no return of symptoms. He also stopped using the SAMe about two months later, and we did see anxiety and low mood return, although not to the original level. Tim felt better about a week after restarting the SAMe. His weight has remained stable.

Tim continues his yoga and SAMe to this day.

Cortisol is a hormone produced by our adrenal glands in response to stress. It is responsible for stress-related weight gain, lowered immune function, and deterioration of the brain. Yoga is a powerful method for lowering cortisol levels, and results can be visible after just one class and even more with regular classes. Because high cortisol levels are associated with depression, it would make sense that yoga should be prescribed as an antidepressant therapy.

MEDITATION AND BREATHING

While depression destroys healthy cells in the brain, meditation can regenerate them. Recent compelling evidence from scientific researchers at Harvard revealed that meditation helps increase the creation and growth of nerves, with forty minutes of deep meditation a day showing the greatest healthy changes in brain structure. The meditators had literally changed their physical brain structure compared with people who didn't meditate. MRI scans show that meditation boosts brain thickness of structures that tend to atrophy with age. It's plausible then that meditation can slow or stop the effects of aging on the brain.

More studies are clearly needed on the benefits of meditation as well as on specific meditative techniques to determine if some are more beneficial for patients with depression. I also recommend meditation if you have strong anxiety. In some cases of low mood, especially when someone is quite sedentary, I recommend moving your body by using a social activity like tai qi or yoga instead of quiet meditation.

SPIRITUALITY AND RELIGION

For most of the twentieth century, the psychiatry field has had a somewhat negative view of spirituality, probably stemming from both Sigmund Freud's antireligious bias as well as the fact that mental illness care during the late nineteenth century focused on brain chemistry and drugs. However, in the past few decades, spirituality has gained increasing recognition as an important aspect of medical and psychiatric care.

Spirituality and association with religion can be a connecting experience or an alienating one. In the most positive light, religion can bring a sense of connection, purpose, hope, and meaning as well as a feeling that people can transcend beyond their physical world to be part of a greater community. I have found that spirituality is clearly important to most patients. In fact, studies show that about 77 percent of patients prefer their physicians talk about spiritual needs. In addition, 48 percent prefer their physicians to pray with them, and 37 percent would like to see their doctor ask them about their religious beliefs. One study showed that 79 percent of people believed that spiritual faith could help with recovery from illness, injury, or disease and that 64 percent thought that physicians should join their patients in prayer if the patient requested it.

Among a group of practicing Christian patients with mild depression, one researcher looked at the effects of adding an emphasis on religious themes to a CBT program and found large reductions in depression. Whether or not the therapist was personally religious made absolutely no difference to the outcome. However, in cases in which no religious association was used, the largest reductions in depression were made by therapists who were personally religious themselves. Simply incorporating religious association into treatment enhanced outcome.

Religion is not necessary to heal from depression, but if you are reading this and you have a past religious affiliation or leaning that was a positive experience, or you have considered joining an organized religious group—I encourage you to consider this further. You will know if a group is right for you. If you do not believe religion is right for you, that is okay too—this book covers many non-religious choices to help you achieve your best mood and health.

CHINESE MEDICINE AND ACUPUNCTURE

Acupuncture is a thousands-year-old treatment based on the system of traditional Chinese medicine (TCM). TCM looks to nature to understand health. It considers the natural world to be full of good energy, and it views disease as an imbalance of energy in our body relative to the natural world's energy (called *qi* and pronounced "chee"). In many cases, disease is stagnant energy, a deficiency of energy or, more rarely, an excess of energy.

In TCM, there's a basic concept of *yin* and *yang*, as expressed in the symbol above. The white areas represent yang, which is full of light, energy, daytime, and movement. Yang represents the male energy, going outward, and heat. The darker area is the yin part, representing quiet, female, nourishment, dark, nighttime, stillness, coolness, and energy in reserve. In your body, yang and yin work together to create harmony, moving in and out of each other all the time. When your body is out of balance, TCM would say that yin and yang are out of harmony—one is taking over the other, either because one is too strong or the other is too weak.

Depression is typically a yin problem, and when it's out of balance, it's the reason why people become very quiet and withdrawn. Depressed people act much more yin. Aspects of life, such as excessive competition and stress, can create this imbalance. As we will learn in chapter 8, twice as many women experience depression than men—women are generally more yin than men are, so they are more prone to depression, especially in high-stress, competitive work environments. As such, it's recommended that women (and sensitive men) protect themselves from that kind of harshness.

Depression, in TCM, is marked by emotional disorder and the stagnation of qi caused by emotional disturbance. The disease is due to accumulated anger, anxiety, sorrow, or other unprocessed emotions that can lead to dysfunction and imbalances in yin and yang. Some say depression can be "anger turned inward." As a result, knotted qi accumulates, and a disruption of the body and mind results.

The emotional issue decides which organ in the body has the most problems. For example, some patients tend toward fear, which can cause a kidney imbalance. Other people have a lot of anger, hostility, or lack of motivation, which are liver issues. Sometimes excessive amounts of sorrow or even happiness attack the heart. Grief and loss affect the lungs.

Practicing in New York City, I have had the honor of working with many people who experienced extreme loss during the 9/11 crisis. As is well documented, many of these people have lung and respiratory problems such as asthma, breathing difficulty, or sarcoidosis. While convention suggests that there must have been unknown particulates in the air causing these lung problems, the TCM practitioner would suggest the incredible amount of loss attacked the lungs to cause these respiratory problems. I have found that acupuncture and Chinese herbs have been valuable in alleviating symptoms while I look closer at the sense of loss to help 9/11 victims move through this grief.

ORGAN	EMOTION
Lungs and colon	Grief and guilt
Liver and gallbladder	Stress and anger
Kidneys and bladder	Fear, anxiety
Stomach and digestion	Worry, rejection
Heart	Joy, sorrow

The Chinese Medicine Organ/Emotion Link

In TCM, any disease, including depression, suggests that your body is out of balance with the energy and influences of the nature around you. These natural influences are categorized as wind, cold, heat, damp, dryness, and summer heat. Too much or too little of these can deplete qi or trap it so it is stuck. The long-term trapping of qi eventually leads to stagnation of qi in an organ. With depression, this results in the body feeling fatigued. Chronic qi stagnation also depletes blood and drains nutrients—a reason I check blood for low levels of vitamin D, B_{12}, and other nutrients. Chronically stuck energy also increases damp, phlegm, and fire in the body and can manifest physically as mucus production, slow digestion, yeast infection, swelling, and heat sensation.

We have spent a good amount of time in this book talking about inflammation. The idea of "damp, phlegm, and fire" correlates well with the modern medical science version of inflammation. In fact, some Chinese texts refer to depression as "phlegm misting the mind." Although TCM might seem worlds away from modern medicine in terms of language, I believe its powerful observation and treatment principles developed over thousands of years is complementary to Western medicine and can sometimes explain what modern medicine fails to describe.

I would like to discuss two organs that are very important in regard to mood and depression. Although every organ can play a role, these two seem to be the most unbalanced. Now, please note that when we talk about an organ, it does not mean that your physical heart or liver necessarily has an organic problem that you will find with a blood test, scan, or biopsy. If you suspect you have a heart problem as described below and decide to see a cardiologist, he will probably not find anything wrong. These descriptions are energetic TCM descriptions of the organ and do not imply an actual physical issue.

The Heart

In TCM, the heart is where the mind and spirit reside. The mind and spirit are also known as the *shen* of a person. So when you meet people who have obvious mental and emotional issues to the point that they seem disconnected from reality (as you might see in someone with psychosis), they have a shen disturbance. Many of these people require drug or psychiatric therapy. Rest assured, most people with emotional issues and depression are not shen disturbed. If you are reading this book, you are likely not shen disturbed. However, we all may still experience some level of blockage of qi in the heart. Remember this is not actual physical blockage in most cases, but blockage of energy movement that relates to spirit in the Chinese medicine tradition.

Your heart is responsible for making decisions about what makes you happy. Many people with heart issues have a lack of dreams or are confused about life's direction. When people decide to follow a career that they know they are not really interested in or decide to do something that is not right for them, they are "going against the heart." Sometimes, people become so accustomed to going against their heart that they do not even notice conflict. But the heart sustains damage every time, and slowly, depression sets in. Henry David Thoreau said, "Most men lead lives of quiet desperation." I think he was referring to people disconnected from their heart.

If you want to work on your heart, a good practice is to review your day and check if you are making decisions that go against your heart. These could be big or small—but each one damages your heart spirit and contributes to depression. As you identify these decisions and start making new ones, you will see mood lift.

The Liver

Your liver is affected greatly by stress and stagnant energy. But the liver is resilient—in fact, you can cut out practically the whole liver, and it will grow back! No other organ can do that. In TCM, the liver is considered the general of the body. It uses willpower to take the heart's instructions and carry them out.

People with a weak liver know what they want to do and what is right for them but cannot do it because the general is not strong. They experience little drive, no determination, lack of steadfastness, low enthusiasm, and minimal physical and mental power. I see this very often with patients who have depression. They know what is good for them and what makes them happy, but they are not motivated to make the changes they need. I find that for these people positivity work, along with acupuncture, can motivate.

Acupuncture

It's the intention of the TCM practitioner to use food, lifestyle, acupuncture, and herbal therapies to move blocked qi and to nourish deficiency when needed in order to return the body and mind to harmony. Although we do not know exactly how acupuncture works, Western medicine has studied it and finds it can stimulate afferent Group III nerves, a type of nerve that transmits impulses to various parts of the central nervous system and induces the release of serotonin, norepinephrine, dopamine, b-endorphin, and other emotion-supporting molecules called enkephalins and dynorphins. Many of these are secreted in the hypothalamus, the middle part of the brain where the nervous, immune, and hormonal systems all meet and coordinate with each other. Hypothalamus changes affect mood. Acupuncture also influences changes in the autonomic nervous system (which governs the ability to get stressed or calm down), the immune system, inflammation, and hormones.

In truth, research studies conflict somewhat regarding the benefits of acupuncture. However, a recent and thorough 2008 meta-analysis of eight trials for 477 patients concluded that acupuncture could significantly reduce the severity of depression. In my own clinic, I find clear benefits using acupuncture in collaboration with conventional medicine. Acupuncture allows the pharmaceutical medications to work quicker and typically allows for a lower dose. Acupuncture is also excellent while a patient is weaning off conventional medications, and it is a very powerful adjunct to use with natural medicines.

Is Acupuncture Safe?

One of the wonderful benefits of acupuncture is that there are virtually no contraindications to treatment, except for the occasional patient who is afraid of needles. Acupuncture does not adversely

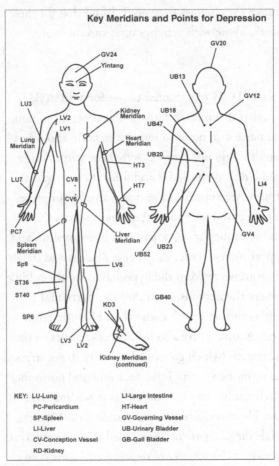

Figure 4: Key Meridians and Points for Depression

interact with other medications or treatments and will not interfere with breast feeding in postpartum women. Two reviews including 350,000 treatments found side effects to be exceedingly rare. In very rare cases, when acupuncture is not administered properly, points used over the chest could cause a lung to deflate—this is something I have never seen happen in the thousands of patients I have worked with. I have seen people feel dizzy or have a panic attack occasionally after a treatment. More commonly, I see people have an emotional release, such as crying, which is often a good thing. For best results and to ensure safety, work with a trained, qualified, licensed practitioner, preferably one who has received a master's degree in acupuncture from an accredited three-year program.

Qi Gong

Qi gong incorporates meditation with a purposeful attempt to nourish and heal the body. According to qi gong principles, you learn to cultivate, store, and move energy to relieve symptoms and encourage healing. So in a way, it's like doing acupuncture on yourself but without using needles. When you are anxious and depressed, you probably breathe in a shallow pattern, which affects the flow of oxygen and energy into your body. The qi gong exercise encourages deep breaths, increasing oxygen levels to your tissues.

In one study, thirty-nine subjects suffering from either major depression, dysthymia, or bipolar disorder were taught a qi gong technique called the Level One Spring Forest Qigong techniques in a one-day training session with two follow-up sessions one and two months later. Supportive audio and video recordings were also given to the volunteers to practice for at least forty minutes each day. Researchers determined that all subjects improved over the treatment period, with the severely depressed subjects improving significantly.

MASSAGE

Massage therapy is one of the most ancient of health care practices. First recorded in Chinese medical texts more than four thousand years old, massage has been advocated outside Asia at least since the time of Hippocrates.

Massage therapy is shown to improve mood, reduce pain perception, balance electric patterns in the brain, and decrease cortisol. Although at this time no formal research has studied massage as a treatment for depression, I believe it's well indicated. Touch is essential to life. Review studies on babies who are held soon after birth versus those who are not showed that the second group went on to have more physical and emotional challenges as children and adults. I believe receiving human touch is important to life from the first day through the last. Massage is a type of therapeutic touch that can be quite effective to help patients with depression and may bring a sea change in emotional health for some people, especially if touch is otherwise minimal in their life.

MANIPULATION

Based on the concept of freeing nerves for optimum health of the body, manipulative therapies like osteopathic and chiropractic work have been used to treat a host of conditions, including depressive illness. There has been relatively little research using manipulative therapies for mood disorder, although anecdotal evidence remains plentiful.

There's one eight-week study of osteopathic manipulative treatment used as an adjunct to standard psychiatric treatment of seventeen premenopausal women with newly diagnosed depression. In this study, 100 percent of the manipulation group and only 33 percent of the control group improved, while neither group had lower inflammation markers. It seemed the manipulation helped the patients feel better but likely not by reducing body inflammation. There's a single case report of a forty-six-year-old man with major depression who received specific chiropractic adjustments and found that his quality of life and wellness increased. Another study focused on fifteen depressed adults treated by a technique called orthospinology, which is a method of correcting upper neck subluxations. It found eleven subjects to have improved mood, while two had minimal improvement and two were worse.

If you are experiencing back and neck symptoms, it's probably worth visiting your chiropractor, naturopath, or osteopathic doctor to see if manipulation can help your mood as well as your back and neck symptoms. Manipulation may not be appropriate for people with low bone density or with advanced stiffness in the arteries of the neck.

CRANIOSACRAL THERAPY

Craniosacral therapy involves gentle manipulation of the head, back bone, and sacrum in order to release tensions and imbalances in the bones and membranes of the skull. While the previous section focused on manipulation with a stronger movement, craniosacral therapy is a much subtler and gentler technique safe enough for babies and osteoporotic women, who should not have regular manipulative work. Craniosacral therapy has shown some benefits for depression as well as for anxiety, headaches, neck and back pain, migraine, and even colicky babies.

Fibromyalgia is a condition characterized by pain, low mood, inflammation, and autonomic system dysfunction. Fibromyalgia and depression may have a number of similarities. In one study, eighty-four patients diagnosed with fibromyalgia were treated with craniosacral therapy for twenty-five weeks and found a significant improvement in their levels of anxiety, pain, quality of life, and sleep quality. More studies are needed, but given the gentle and non-risk nature of the treatment, I would recommend considering this as a mood-improvement option for anyone.

EMOTIONAL FREEDOM TECHNIQUE

Emotional Freedom Technique (EFT) is a therapy that uses finger tapping on acupuncture points combined with a type of talk therapy in order to reprogram negative thinking patterns. In many cases, it can help accelerate the process of reaching underlying issues for patients. Successful application has been observed to treat phobias, and my personal experience with this simple technique has generally yielded mild to significant results in approximately 70 percent of patients experiencing grief, pain, guilt, anxiety, stuck emotion, and functional digestive illness.

This technique involves creating a particular phrase that addresses the emotional blockage and then moving through a series of repetitive statements around that phrase while simultaneously tapping on acupuncture points. My first experience with EFT was as a student clinician in medical school. I was working with my colleague Dr. Fred Shotz, who had decided to become a doctor after years as an airline pilot. He learned EFT in order to help his passengers who had airplane phobias learn to traverse this fear and get on an airplane. During our first visit with a patient, I witnessed Shotz help a woman who had found nothing that would help her breathing problems. The EFT helped her realize her history as a questionable mother was a core problem, and I was very impressed with her physical results: she started breathing in a relaxed manner within a week, even after every steroid and drug had had no effect. I learned from that session that some issues are beyond the pharmaceutical realm. Even though I didn't fully understand why the EFT worked, I knew that this was powerful medicine.

Today, I use EFT with patients, and I teach many of them to continue to use it for their own self-care. To date, no formal research has studied EFT for patients with depression. More free information is readily available at *www.eftuniverse.com*.

BIOFEEDBACK

There's an old Chinese proverb that says, "Tension is who you think you should be. Relaxation is who you are." Biofeedback can help create relaxation out of tension. Founded in 1961 by experimental psychologist Neal Miller, biofeedback involves the practitioner using a monitoring machine to instruct patients on how to control the part of the nervous system that runs the stress and relaxation systems of our body (called the autonomic nervous system). Also known as applied psychophysiological feedback, biofeedback focuses on gaining control over involuntary functions such as heart rate, blood pressure, skin temperature, and muscle tension in order to improve health and well-being. Neurofeedback is a specific type of biofeedback that specializes in reading and altering brain waves (delta, theta, alpha, and beta) to achieve a therapeutic effect.

Two open-label (meaning the subjects knew the treatment they were getting) trials have shown positive results with depressed patients using biofeedback. One ten-week study from the University of Medicine and Dentistry of New Jersey found that eleven subjects had significant improvements in depression and in their heart's ability to adapt during the treatment period. Heart adaptability refers to the nervous system being balanced. A German open-label study showed mood elevation and much less depression. Additional benefits included reduced anxiety, lowered heart rate, and ability of the heart rate to properly adjust its rate after conduction of biofeedback. No changes were found in the control subjects.

Finally, other studies with larger groups of depressed patients with cardiovascular disease have also reported similar results. Cardiac patients taking antidepressants place themselves at greater risk, likely because serotonin and norepinephrine reuptake inhibitors can also diminish heart rate variability. With no known risks, biofeedback seems to be an effective and safe alternate treatment that may be especially useful for cardiac patients with depression.

ART THERAPY

Art therapy is the therapeutic use of creating art by people who have experienced illness, trauma, or challenges, and also by people who seek personal growth and development. By making art and subsequently reflecting on the work, patients can increase awareness of self and others and learn how to cope with symptoms, stress, and even traumatic experience. Also, art therapy is known to enhance brain function and foster the life-affirming pleasures of making art.

Expression of depression and other painful feelings via art therapy can help depressed patients process their feelings and resolve conflict. It's thought that art therapy can reactivate the nondominant hemisphere of the brain. Particularly in chronic or recurrent depression cases, this reactivation may serve to open a person up to new perspectives and solutions to the challenges that encourage depressive feelings.

MUSIC THERAPY

As a drummer since age eleven, I can attest to music's ability to calm and improve mood (although as I was a teenager with a drum set in the house, I am not so sure all that noise made my parents feel so relaxed). One large study in Finland has recently verified what I already learned: that music has a clear benefit on mood and quality of life. This analysis looked at thirty studies covering 1,891 patients with cancer. Cancer may arguably be one of the most difficult stressors a person can face. Using music therapy, or prerecorded music, these patients showed beneficial effects on heart rate, respiratory rate, and blood pressure. Previous studies report that music helps decrease anxiety before and during surgical and chemotherapy procedures, reduce side effects of cancer treatment, help mood, decrease pain, boost the immune system, and improve life quality.

Even more to our subject, music therapy has been shown to help depression when added to standard antidepressant treatments. Another study by the same Finnish researchers looked at twenty biweekly sessions of music therapy for thirty-three depressed patients of working age (eighteen to fifty years) using conventional drugs, while another forty-six patients just used conventional drug therapy. According to the researchers:

> Music therapy offers an alternative and is another way to get in touch with emotions and develop relationships without relying on talking and verbally expressing feelings, which can be hard for some people. . . . Moreover, you don't have to be a musician nor musically talented in order to get benefit from this treatment.

The music therapy consisted of one-on-one sessions with a music therapist, in which the patients were free to make music with drums and a xylophone, followed by discussion. After ninety days, the volunteers who received music therapy had clearly greater improvement than those who only took the drugs.

The researchers also noticed that music therapy dropout rate was very low and the commitment level was very high, probably because people were having fun.

* * *

Congratulations on making it through chapter 6. We briefly discussed a few forms of psychotherapy as well as a number of treatments that I myself would have thought a bit "out there" before I learned about the practical and effective benefits of natural healing. You certainly will not need to use all of these modalities (at least not at the same time), but I would like you to think about the ones we discussed and see which ones resonate with you the most. They may not all make sense to you from an intellectual standpoint, but do your best to open up aspects of your spirit that go beyond sense; rely on intuition, for this can help guide you to which methods to try first.

PART III

Meds, Gender, and Seniors

7

If You're on Medication, Read This!

If you are on medication right now, it's important to continue it, especially if it is helping you feel better.

Remember, it's never a good or safe idea to simply stop taking antidepressant medication. We will talk about how to safely wean off at the appropriate time with your doctor's monitoring at the end of this chapter. But for now, do not change a thing about your medications.

However, if your medications are not helping you, or you believe the side effects are greater than the benefits, it's important you speak to your prescribing doctor now about some alternatives. In the meantime, the natural remedies covered in this chapter are backed up by solid research to support your life with medication, either to make it work better or to help avoid side effects.

SUPPLEMENTS TO SUPPORT YOUR MEDICATION

Because you are on medication, the first thing to think about is making sure the medication is working best for you. I have worked with scores of patients who have come in on medications (often-times two or three) and have told me that the medications have not been working, their psychiatrists are seemingly randomly taking them off one and putting them on another, and they are still not getting any better. Patients have also told me that medications did work for a time but then stopped working and they don't know what to do. The first thing I think of is to use some of the natural nutrients below, which can jump-start a medication regimen and get you feeling better.

Folic Acid

In the field of medicine, I have noticed that the more medication choices there are for a condition, the less any of them are likely to work. This is very true for depression.

About 70 percent of depressed patients do not experience an elevated mood when given medication. As a result, these patients are run through a series of adjunctive, or add-on, drugs (like antipsychotic medications) in the hopes of finding a combination that will help the depressed person feel better. These secondary medications boast a paltry 20 to 30 percent success rate (also known as 70 to 80 percent failure rate). One proven way to avoid this is by taking folate.

One 2000 study of 127 patients found that 500 mcg of folic acid taken daily with Prozac greatly improved the drug's effect. A more recent folate study looked at seventy-five patients who were already taking antidepressant medication but were not respond-ing. It was shown that patients taking 15 mg of folate per day (which is a high amount for this vitamin) found their medication to work significantly better—and these effects were as good or bet-ter than the added conventional medications studied, according to the authors. These studies suggest that this simple B vitamin may be a viable alternative to the vast array of adjunctive medications, including antipsychotic medications like Abilify or even antiepilep-tic meds like Lamictal.

In my opinion, it makes sense that when possible, patients already using medication should augment their therapy with natural solutions instead of layering on another pharmaceutical. If you are on medications, take a total of 15 mg of folate a day in the methyl-folate form. Look for the methyl-folate version of this nutrient, which is more natural than other versions. More about folate can be found in chapter 5.

Zinc

Like our B vitamin friend, zinc may be a valuable ally if you are using medication that simply is not working.

One study looked at the effect of zinc deprivation on antidepressant drugs. The researchers gave some mice a zinc-deficient diet, while control mice had a normal diet. Then, they gave animals a stressor (called the forced swim test) to induce depression. They found that the animals who were zinc deprived had a minimal response to the antidepressant, whereas the animals with plenty of zinc in their body were much more able to respond positively when given medication.

Is it possible that antidepressants could be engineered to work well, but the reason they are not effective in so many people is because we are a nutrient-depleted society?

Animal studies show positive results, but mice and humans are very different creatures. How do we know this zinc issue is important in humans?

One group of researchers asked that very question and gave a daily dose of 25 mg of zinc to six patients on antidepressants, while the control group of eight patients was given standard antidepressant drug therapy only. Each patient's sense of well-being was evaluated before the treatment and then up to twelve weeks after. Within six weeks, patients taking zinc reported elevated mood, while those who didn't take the extra zinc did not.

This was a small study, but given the safety of zinc and its possible benefit, I highly recommend you add 25 mg of zinc to your regimen. If you are taking zinc for more than a few months, please make sure you are taking 2 mg of copper per day (often found in a good multiple vitamin), for extra zinc can decrease copper levels in your body over the long term. More about zinc can be found in chapter 5.

Vitamin B$_{12}$

One study looked at serum vitamin B$_{12}$ levels in 115 people taking medication for major depressive disorder. It's interesting, for none of the patients in this study had deficient vitamin B$_{12}$ levels—meaning all patients were in normal range for the vitamin. In the group of forty patients who weren't responding to medication, the average vitamin B$_{12}$ level was 470.5 pg/mL (normal range is 200 pg/mL to 1,100 pg/mL). Of the thirty-four people who had a partial response to medication, the average vitamin B$_{12}$ level was 536.6 pg/mL. The forty-one people who reported a full response to medication had an average vitamin B$_{12}$ measurement of 594.9 pg/mL. It's clear from this study that the higher the vitamin B$_{12}$ level, the better the patient outcome. This suggests to me that all my patients with depression should have a B$_{12}$ level of at least 600 pg/mL, even though most doctors would be happy with a level over 200 pg/mL. Many blood tests even state that people with levels between 200 and 400 may show neuropsychiatric problems, so looking for 600 pg/mL or higher makes a lot of sense. I know of no reason to worry about B$_{12}$ toxicity, even at levels around 1200 pg/mL.

If you are taking medication, you can ask a doctor for intramuscular B$_{12}$ shots once a week, or if you prefer oral doses, I recommend the methylcobalamin version, starting at 10,000 mcg once a day, which is about ten times the daily maintenance dose recommended in chapter 5. Please check your blood B$_{12}$ levels in one month to look for a change. If there's no change, you can increase the dose, and you may also want to consider improving your diet to help digestion and absorption (see chapter 3). More about B$_{12}$ can be learned in chapter 5.

Testosterone

We discussed the importance of this hormone way back in chapter 4 when discussing blood tests. Testosterone may be even more beneficial in patients who are already taking medications but are not experiencing good results.

In a small, eight-week study, nineteen men taking medication for depression were given either 10 g of transdermal (through the skin) testosterone gel per day or an equivalent amount of placebo cream. These men had not responded well to drugs and also had low or normal testosterone levels. The testosterone-treated patients reported a significant decrease in depression than the placebo-treated patients.

I have seen many cases of healthy mood adjustments using a little testosterone in both men and women. I find that low-testosterone patients often have a bit of hard-to-lose belly fat and have low or irritable mood. Even women should have testosterone checked, and if it's low, talk to your doctor about taking a small amount to see if your mood improves. Have your doctor recheck your levels in a month or two.

Thyroid Hormone

In chapter 4, we talked about the multiple ways thyroid hormone helps the mind and body of a person with depression. Thyroid hormone may also be an ally to medication that is otherwise not working.

As early as 1969, astute researchers showed that when patients on tricyclic antidepressants were given a form of thyroid hormone called triiodothyronine (T3), the result was an "enhanced and accelerated recovery." Since that time, it has been shown that 55 to 60 percent of patients who previously failed to respond to tricyclic antidepressants experienced an improvement with thyroid hormone.

In one study of almost three hundred patients, those treated with T3, or a more natural glandular thyroid support, ranging from 20 to 50 mcg per day were twice as likely to respond than to placebo and almost three times more likely to respond than to thyroxine (T4).

There were also a few studies in which T3 was used successfully when given to patients who were also taking serotonin reuptake inhibitor medications. It was shown in these studies that lack of energy was common in patients given Prozac, but when the T3 was added, the low energy went away, with no side effects noted.

CLINICAL CASE: TRISH'S T3

Trish was a fifty-four-year-old patient coming in for constipation, high cholesterol, some weight gain, fatigue, and depression. She had bounced around from antidepressant to antidepressant since menopause eight years ago, finding little benefit. She had been on Zoloft for the past year, and her latest psychopharmacologist recommended adding Lamictal to the mix.

As soon as I heard her symptoms, I started to think about the thyroid. I asked Trish whether she felt cold or had dry skin regularly, but she denied it: "I tend to feel hot most of the time, and my skin is good as long as I put skin cream on every day." So she was not cold, but I suspected dry skin, which is a symptom of low thyroid. I asked for her past laboratory tests, which she faxed to me. Her TSH level was 2.9, with her total T4 and T3 in very low-normal ranges. "My doctor said my thyroid is just fine," she said. I suggested to her it might not be fine, and in fact it may be a factor in all her symptoms. I asked her for a full thyroid panel (see chapter 4), and it revealed that her T4 and T3 were low (T4 and T3 are the main thyroid hormones in the body that are responsible for help with cell metabolism, heat generation, healthy skin, and an effective mind). I suggested Trish try natural thyroid replacement and see how she felt.

Within two weeks, her constipation was gone and her depression symptoms had been improved 85 percent. We added some cod liver oil, thyroid supportive herbs and nutrients, and homeopathic Sepia and even got her to start morning walks outside. In six months, she reported to me that her weight was down, her skin didn't need cream, her energy was higher, and her cholesterol was normal.

If you are on medications that are not working well, ask your doctor to check your thyroid levels. If they are okay, but on the lower to normal side, you may want to ask for a small dose of T3 (called Cytomel) or a natural glandular thyroid like Armour Thyroid, and to have your levels rechecked regularly. Your doctor may insist on using T4 (also known as thyroxine). You can refer to this book to guide a discussion with your doctor.

The discussion about thyroid hormone in chapter 4 also talks about nonhormonal ways to support thyroid if you would like to use those first. When taking thyroid hormone, always look for signs of too much hormone. These can show up as a fast heart rate, sweating, and greasy skin and hair as well as in anxiety symptoms.

Estrogen

In some post menopausal women being treated for depression, estrogen replacement therapy has been shown to improve the effects of conventional antidepressants. If you are a post menopausal woman who is struggling with medications that do not work for you, please read the hormone discussion in chapter 8.

Ginkgo

This wonderful herb will be discussed further in chapter 8 for its benefits in the senior population. In this chapter, I want to discuss ginkgo specifically in relationship to helping common side effects of antidepressants: loss of sexual drive and low libido, which occur in 43 percent of men and women taking SSRIs.

Patients are known to experience sexual dysfunction with antidepressant medications. In an open trial, ginkgo extract was found to be 84 percent effective in treating antidepressant-induced sexual dysfunction. In this study, women were found to be more responsive to the sexually enhancing effects of ginkgo than men, although both enjoyed its benefit, with success rates of 91 percent and 76 percent, respectively. Ginkgo biloba generally had a positive effect on all four phases of the sexual response cycle: desire, excitement (including erection and lubrication), orgasm, and resolution (the afterglow or good feeling immediately following orgasm).

Dosage and Toxicity of Ginkgo

I recommend starting ginkgo at 40 mg of the extract (standardized to 24 percent ginkgo flavonglycosides) three times a day. If no change is noticeable in two weeks, increase dosage to 80 mg three times a day. The standardization means that about 24 percent of the total amount of ginkgo should be made up of the flavonglycoside component. A good quality company usually lists this information on the label. Although the level of flavonglycosides is important, also remember to use an extract that includes the whole ginkgo leaf, for we do not know exactly what parts of the ginkgo actually help with mood and sexual side effects.

Ginkgo biloba leaf extract is quite low in toxicity, but this supplement should be avoided if you are taking diabetes medications, anticlotting medications, or antiepileptic drugs. Find a full description of ginkgo in chapter 8.

Yohimbe

From the coffee plant family, *Pausinystalia yohimbe* contains an alkaloid named yohimbine, which is well known for the treatment of erectile problems and impotence.

Medical research is starting to look into this herb for depression. In fact, my former employer, the National Institute of Mental Health, currently has a trial on the effect of yohimbe as an antidepressant underway. This study will assess the efficacy of a single dose of intravenous yohimbine compared with placebo in improving overall depression symptoms when administered during sleep. I am very interested to see how it turns out and whether oral forms will work too.

Yohimbe also seems to possess the ability to help medicated patients respond more quickly and better to SSRI medications. One randomized, controlled trial of fifty patients with a diagnosis of major depressive disorder showed that subjects who took Prozac plus a titrated dose of yohimbine responded more rapidly than those who took Prozac alone. Titration means the dose was slowly increased while monitoring patients for blood pressure changes. You should know that one real concern about yohimbine and the yohimbe plant is that its powerful effect on the nervous system can not only improve mood and sexual feeling, but it can also raise blood pressure. Dosage needs to be watched carefully. Right now, we do not know what demographic is more inclined to experience high blood pressure as a side effect, so each person taking yohimbe needs to be careful.

Yohimbe is known for helping with the sexual side effects of antidepressant medications due to its ability to block receptors called presynaptic alpha-2 adrenergic receptors. When these are blocked, our adrenergic tone (healthy nervous response) is enhanced, allowing for a robust sexual response.

One study of five patients with either obsessive compulsive disorder, trichotillomania (obsessive hair pulling), anxiety, or affective disorders like depression who suffered sexual side effects after treatment with SSRIs were given yohimbine on an as-needed basis. All five patients experienced improved sexual functioning after taking yohimbine. In the largest known study, seventeen of twenty-one patients showed improvement of sexual side effects when treated with yohimbine at an average dose of 16.2 mg. That is a pretty significant response.

Dosage and Toxicity of Yohimbe

Yohimbe does not have any depression research completed at this point, so I do not directly recommend it as an antidepressant therapy. But it may help medications work better and alleviate sexual side effects including low libido.

Yohimbine studies have dosed anywhere from 2.7 mg to 16.2 mg daily, usually divided into three daily doses. Another choice is using an herbal tincture with a concentration of 1:5 giving a range of 5 to 20 drops three times a day. The amounts of yohimbine in these liquid preparations may vary, so it is best to start at a low dose and work up as needed.

Please note: If you are experiencing sexual side effects, I strongly recommend trying ginkgo before using yohimbe. If you use ginkgo for two months and still do not see a benefit, then consider a low yohimbe dose. If you decide to take yohimbe, you should work with a naturopathic physician, qualified herbalist, or other practitioner experienced with this herb—and let your prescribing medical doctor know you are using it as well. As described, it's best to start at low doses and titrate to a therapeutic dose to avoid side effects and then keep monitoring your blood pressure daily. Possible side effects of yohimbe included higher blood pressure, excessive sweating, increased anxiety, and a wound-up feeling. This is not an herb to use lightly—be respectful of this one.

DUMPING THE MEDS

After reading this book, you may think, Okay, I am ready to stop my medications. That is a wonderful goal to move toward—but it's important to remember that until you bring in the recommendations in this book and make the necessary changes in your body and spirit, simply stopping your medications may not help you feel any better, especially if you are in the 30 percent of patients who benefit from using antidepressants. Also, if you're experiencing severe depression, it's important to remember that it may be best to take medication for the longer term while working with natural supplements.

Getting off antidepressants is like getting off any drug—there's a withdrawal that has its own set of symptoms. These can include confusion, irritability, dizziness, lack of coordination, sleeping problems, crying spells, and blurry vision. I have seen patients who have unfortunately stopped their own medications cold turkey or could not get ahold of a refill in time. Believe me when I tell you, they were not happy people. While the drug companies and medical community call these withdrawal symptoms "discontinuation syndrome," we should call it what it is: drug withdrawal.

Antidepressant withdrawal evokes a major behavioral stress response and can cause neurological damage. Improper withdrawal of medications causes greater neurological damage, which can even decrease benefits of future treatments. Getting off medications requires a plan. Please read on with me to learn about that plan.

One thing I have learned through my research and clinical practice is that conventional doctors and psychiatrists are well trained and very good at placing people on medications but are not at all trained or focused on helping people get off their medications. Oftentimes, patients with depression may be left with no choice but to stay on medication. As I have said before, I am not antidrug, for in certain severe circumstances, medications may be an appropriate life-saving choice. However, even in these cases, a post-crisis exit strategy should be discussed from the start.

You should also know that, as with any addictive medicine, people who start antidepressants—whether they have a mood disorder or not—have a very, very challenging time getting off these drugs. Our brains and bodies become dependent on them and withdrawing without negative experience is nearly impossible.

If you have thought about, or even tried, getting off medications but could not due to side effects or a return of the original symptoms, do not fear—I have a plan for you.

Step 1: Don't Change a Thing

Do not try to get off medications without first speaking to your prescribing doctor. I am glad you are reading this book, but I do not know your personal story. As such, I want you to work with someone who knows your situation to make sure your symptoms are within a realm of safety to get off the drug. Some people with severe depression need to stay on medications longer than they sometimes think. And some patients with complicated medical conditions like schizophrenia, bipolar, or other medical issues may not be able to stop taking them at this time. So please, check with your prescribing doctor to make sure you are ready.

When my patients and I talk about this, a number of them say, "But I can't talk to my doctor." If you do not feel like you have a good relationship with your particular doctor, then start looking for another one with whom you're comfortable speaking. Remember, your health is on the line, and you deserve someone whom you can spend time with and speak honestly to. There are many gentle, caring psychiatrists out there too. You may need to interview a few, but you will find one that is right for you.

Step 2: Follow the Naturopathic Path

Follow the quick guide to the naturopathic path in chapter 2 and then start the naturopathic recommendations that apply to you as laid out in the other chapters (learn which in chapter 1). You will start to change foods, lifestyle, stress responses, sleep, nutrients, botanicals, and more. If you do not make changes to prepare your body for stopping antidepressants, you cannot expect your body to be able to wean off medications.

As a general rule, follow your regimen for at least four months. What I find is typically, after two months, my patients who are still on medications start to talk to me about the idea of not needing their medications anymore. That means there has been some shift in their body and consciousness, and we can get started on the road to safely weaning off the medications. This shift is not always tangible, but when it happens, you will know. I usually recommend once you have added the recommended naturopathic remedies and feel that shift, wait at least another month or two to make sure that shift holds and is a real change.

Step 3: Supplement to Support the Medication Weaning Process

This is the step in which we add a few things to help your body get up to neurotransmitter speed. The general idea is to consider which medications you are taking and then to gently support your body by giving it the precursors to the neurotransmitters that the drugs already support.

I strongly recommend you do this only after starting the other naturopathic therapies discussed in this book. Once you feel your body and mind are in a significantly healthier place, you can then begin the following supplement and drug-weaning schedule. Please work with the knowledge and support of your prescribing doctor. Have your doctor help create the best schedule for slowly tapering any medications.

The following chart lists medications and the related naturopathic support to help your body create its own neurotransmitters. These supplements are like little stairs that help you go down a steep decline so you can avoid the icy ramp. These amino acids and herbs put out little steps for your nervous and hormonal system to brace themselves as they move down the path to a medication-free life.

Natural Supports for Weaning Off Medication

IF YOU ARE READY TO WEAN OFF PRESCRIPTION DRUGS	USE THESE SUPPLEMENTS FOR AT LEAST TWO MONTHS BEFORE ATTEMPTING TO TAPER WITH YOUR DOCTOR'S HELP
SSRIs: Citalopram (Celexa) Escitalopram (Lexapro) Fluoxetine (Prozac, Prozac Weekly, Sarafem) Paroxetine (Paxil, Paxil CR, Pexeva) Sertraline (Zoloft)	5-HTP: 50 mg each day for one week, then 50 mg twice a day for three weeks OR Tryptophan: 500 mg once a day in the evening for the first week, then 500 mg both in the late afternoon and before bed for weeks two through four Take any of the above for two months before starting to wean off medications.
SSRI/SSNRI Combination Drugs: Venlafaxine (Effexor) Desvenlafaxine (Pristiq) Duloxetine (Cymbalta) Milnacipran (Savella, Ixel)	Tyrosine: 500 mg once a day for two weeks, then 500 mg twice a day for two more weeks THEN ADD 5-HTP: 50 mg a day Take for two months before starting to wean medications.

IF YOU ARE READY TO WEAN OFF PRESCRIPTION DRUGS	USE THESE SUPPLEMENTS FOR AT LEAST TWO MONTHS BEFORE ATTEMPTING TO TAPER WITH YOUR DOCTOR'S HELP
Tricyclic Antidepressants: Amitriptyline (Elavil, Endep, Vanatrip) Amoxapine (Asendin) Desipramine (Norpramin) Doxepin (Adapin, Silenor, Sinequan) Imipramine (Tofranil, Tofranil-PM) Maprotiline (Ludiomil) Nortriptyline (Pamelor) Protriptyline (Vivactil) Trimipramine (Surmontil)	Week one add: Ginkgo: 80 mg per day for one week THEN ADD Tyrosine: 500 mg per day for one week, THEN ADD 5-HTP: 50 mg once a day Take all three of these for a total of two months or more before starting to wean off medications.
Others Bupropion (Wellbutrin, Zyban)	Mucuna Pruriens: 200 mg once a day for two weeks, then 200 mg twice a day after starting the weaning process. Once you are off the medication completely and feeling good for two weeks, take 200 mg once a day for one month then 200 mg every other day for one month. Then discontinue the mucuna completely.
Aripiprazole (Abilify)	Mucuna Pruriens: 200 mg per day for two weeks THEN ADD 5-HTP: 50 mg once a day Take for two months before starting to wean off medication.
Mirtazapine (Remeron)	Tyrosine: 500 mg once a day for two weeks, then 500 mg twice a day for two more weeks Then add: 5-HTP: 50 mg a day Take for two months before starting to wean off medication.

Remember to ask your doctor to help you wean off the medications for a minimum of two months. The longer the tapering period, the better. For people who have been on medications for several years, it may take six to twelve months to taper properly. There's no hurry here. It's best to go as slow as possible. If your prescribing physician would like to go even slower, then that is just fine. Weaning off too quickly from the drug can never help—your body's own ability to make neurotransmitters needs time to start doing its job. The above supplement recommendations should help that process. Even when you do not need the medication anymore, weaning off too quickly will negatively affect your brain's ability to make you happy. Also, when you add a supplement, if something does not feel right or any symptoms get worse, you may want to avoid taking that particular supplement as part of the regimen. You can find these individual supplements in a quality health food store or online, or you may order the ones I use with my patients at www.drpeterbongiorno.com.

During the weaning process, I strongly recommend scheduling regular acupuncture once or twice a week to help your energy balance as the responsibility for your neurotransmitter production is claimed by your body. Acupuncture can be invaluable to help this process. Also, please be aware that as you move towards the lower doses of medication, it may be appropriate to increase one or more of the supplements by a dose. Remember, to continue to work with your doctor during this time, and if you have any unsafe, difficult, or unexpected feelings, please discuss this with your doctor. I have seen many people do very well with this process, but each individual may need slightly more individualized care or schedules for change.

Serotonin Syndrome

When you employ 5-HTP, tryptophan, or Saint-John's-wort with antidepressant medications, or even with each other, some people are concerned about serotonin syndrome. This is a situation in which combined SSRI drugs or a single SSRI drug paired with natural therapies might increase serotonin levels when used together. This syndrome can be characterized by severe agitation, nausea, confusion, hallucinations, fast heartbeat, feeling hot and flushing, coordination issues, hyper reflexes, or gastrointestinal tract symptoms like nausea, vomiting, and diarrhea. Severe cases can cause rapid fluctuation of temperature and blood pressure, mental status changes, and even coma.

Although research shows that giving too many pharmaceutical medications has caused cases of serotonin syndrome, there have been no reports of natural substances causing this syndrome to date, and I have not seen this in my practice using the doses described in this book. Of course, it's best to tell your prescribing physician that you are working with these supplements so you can both carefully monitor your progress and catch any unlikely side effects.

Step 4: Wean Off the Supplements

Well, I do not want you to stay on supplements forever either. Although they are probably safer than pharmaceuticals in the long term, a healthy body should be able to sustain itself with food, water, sleep, exercise, and a balanced spiritual life. So once you are off your medications, wait two more months and then start removing the supplements weekly, just as you added them in. Patients do not tend to experience withdrawal when they wean off the amino acids and herbs, but if you feel you do, you can stay on them as long as you need, for the side effects are minimal to none when used at these dosages.

Step 5: Go Out and Live Your Life, and Keep Up Your Naturopathic Lifestyle

Remember that diet, lifestyle, exercise, doing what makes you happy, meditating, keeping positive messages in your brain, and all the other positive changes you have brought into your life are what really keep you healthy in your mind, body, and spirit. These are core needs for your body that should never be weaned off.

If you start feeling some recurrence of mood symptoms at any point in the future, it's likely your body's way of saying something is not in balance. Please come back to this book, review the changes you made that worked, and get back on that plan. Once you are back on track with these, your body will respond. Please see the Individualized Recommendation List at the end of this book for a complete list of recommendations in this book. Take some time now to check off what you have been doing, what has been working well, and what you need to keep in mind for the future.

Here's a great chance to give you some applause. In psychiatry, most doctors are not well versed in using natural remedies to help drugs work their best, and they are even less versed in helping people get off medications. With this chapter, you have learned how to use natural medicine to allow your body to get the most out of your medications. Even further, you have learned how to support your body naturally in the challenging process of saying goodbye to the drugs. Bravo.

8

Gender and Aging

As far as I'm concerned, being any gender is a drag.

—Patti Smith

Although both men and women are all still from the same planet at this point in human evolution, there are clear differences regarding why each gender can become depressed, how they experience depression, and what it takes to overcome it. My hope with this chapter is to help you refine your depression remedies by learning how your gender influences your depression.

Men and women clearly have different predispositions to psychiatric and emotional issues. Alcoholism, antisocial personality (which is defined as a pattern of disregard for the rights of others), and suicide are more common in men than in women. However, 50 percent more females get depression than males. Along with depression, anxiety, eating disorders, and attempted suicide are also more common in women.

Suicide and Gender

Regarding gender and suicide, about four times as many men kill themselves as do women. So any man with depression needs to be especially monitored. However, it is equally important to remember that suicide attempts are more common in women. This could be because women are more likely to look for support earlier in the depressive process and use a suicide attempt either consciously or subconsciously as a way to reach out. As a note to my fellow doctors out there, physician suicide rates are higher than people in other professions or the general population, and doctors show suicide rates equally divided between men and women. This is a reminder that no one is immune to the ravages of depression.

Remember, if you are considering taking your life, please immediately visit a hospital, psychiatrist, or other practitioner and explain what you are thinking. Medical professionals can and want to help you. This is where modern medicine and drugs can really help, so please take advantage of this care.

Blood, Sugar, and Gender

Overall, the stress hormone cortisol is higher in females. Poor blood sugar control, which can be worsened by cortisol, may affect women more than men. This suggests that women may need to pay more attention to blood sugar by checking it with a test (see chapter 4), eating frequent small meals, consuming plenty of protein (see chapter 3), and possibly adding natural remedies such as chromium and cinnamon, which are known to help the body balance blood sugar levels (chapter 5).

Marriage and Gender

Although hormones are obvious factors in the differences between men and women, emotional and environmental factors, like marriage, can also make us react differently than the opposite sex. Stable, happy marriages tend to create healthy mood. Difficulty in marriage relationships is not only a risk factor for depression, but it has also been found to be a predictor of poor participation in and expectation of therapy. People in unhappy marriages do not tend to respond well to depression treatment, regardless of the type, and are more likely to relapse. Divorce raises the risk of depression by 40 percent. In fact, many women I have worked with to wean them off antidepressant medications started these while going through divorce proceedings as a way to deal with the difficult situation. The problem is, the feelings and coping mechanisms that are covered up by the meds still need to be addressed when the medications are removed.

Ongoing household issues also contribute to mood problems, and vice versa, having a depressed spouse can contribute to marital dissatisfaction, separation, and divorce. Marital therapy attended by both partners, as either a primary or maintenance treatment, can be an important step toward healing. I highly recommend couples counseling if both partners are open to this. A good counselor doesn't necessarily set a goal of saving the marriage but instead helps each person by teaching communication tools so they can figure out what is really best for each person, treating each other kindly and respectfully in the process, no matter the outcome.

Social Situations and Gender

Animal studies that mimic human social predicaments have taught us much about what stresses men versus women. I have compiled the most valuable research and applied it to identify stressors in my patients and to offer changes when possible. Review the following list to see which stressors apply to you.

Crowds

Crowded situations induce social stress in male rats, whereas females are not strongly affected by this condition. I see repeatedly that men can get very stressed when having to deal with crowds on a regular basis. What this means is that maybe a retail job in a busy department store may not be the best place for a man who is prone to depression.

One of my male patients was a manager at Macy's on 34th Street in New York, and as Christmastime neared, he started to get depressed. Although his psychiatrist told him he had seasonal affective disorder, by talking to him about his experience at work, I realized throngs of people were the reason. At first, I thought maybe he was a bit agoraphobic, meaning he was simply afraid of crowds. But as we talked, it sounded more like depression—the crowding induced his low mood. We opened him up to the idea of taking a different job in the company. Once he took a position in office administration and didn't have to deal with the crowds, his depression didn't come back.

Defeat

When one rat is pitted against another, defeated males become despondent, whereas female rats are not so affected by defeat. Studies regarding the economic crisis these past few years have seen an increase in male depression and suicide in Western nations. It's likely that this financial defeat weighs heavily on men. If you are a man with depression, ask yourself: Where in my life do I experience conflict and feel like I lose? These situations could be with a boss, a competitor, an in-law, a savings account that is dwindling, or many other forms of defeat.

How can you change this reaction? Write these situations down, and start to think of them as guides. For instance, if you were a boxer and were defeated after twelve rounds, you would want to look at the video to learn what your opponent did to win and what you could do better the next time. The old saying that "it's only a mistake if you have not learned from it" applies here. Each loss can be a winning situation when we take what we need from it and change our habits for the better.

Social Instability

Some studies regularly switched rats from cage to cage so that none of the rats were able to spend much time with each other or acclimate to their social environment. This was very stressful to the female rats, whereas male rats didn't care much.

If you are a woman in a work or home environment that is not stable, think about ways to change your situation to bring a sense of regularity. Sometimes there are other opportunities regarding places to live or work that might be more in line with your emotional needs. Other studies in humans have also shown that changing sexual partners is generally more stressful for women, but not as much of a stress issue in men.

Isolation

Animal studies showed that keeping an animal away from the rest of the group led to depressive behavior in females much more than in males. Applying this to people, it seems that living alone is quite taxing on women. If you are a woman who lives on your own, I recommend looking into community involvement, volunteering, and social activity as a way to balance the sense of isolation that can affect some women. In the long term, a roommate or housemate may help the situation.

SPECIFICALLY FOR WOMEN

Years ago, when I was a young research assistant at the National Institutes of Health, I asked my mentor why all our experiments were performed with male rats, not females. He said female hormones were very complicated and would confuse research results, so it was simpler not to use females. I learned later that this is also why most research in humans with conditions such as cardiovascular disease is done with men—at the expense of properly treating the disease in women. My hope with this section is to explain what these differences are, and how to use them to our advantage when treating depression.

Birth Control Pills

Ten to 15 percent of women of reproductive age develop a major depressive disorder—which is slightly higher than the general population's 8 to 10 percent. If you are a woman using birth control pills (BCP), you should know that these little pills are notorious for depleting a woman's body of a number of vitamins and for lowering brain serotonin and norepinephrine function as well. As a result, BCP can play a role in contributing to depression. As far as vitamins are concerned, one of the most notable casualties is vitamin B_6, which is needed as a cofactor to manufacture neurotransmitters. Zinc and iron levels are also known to drop, which may also play a role in depression. While not discussed in the literature, my guess is that extra hormonal processing through the liver due to the BCP leads to deficiency by using up valuable vitamins like B_6.

Speaking purely as a naturopathic physician, my preference for my patients would be not to use BCP, especially if they are having mood issues. In a few cases, discontinuation alone helped my patients' low mood. Of course, I also understand that each woman needs to decide what is best and most practical regarding her life. Consider talking to your doctor about other birth control options to see if another is right for you. You may learn about other choices that you could be interested in later even if they are not best for your life situation right now. The idea is to keep yourself educated about your choices and to keep the option of using something other than BCP open.

If you decide to take or continue using BCP, then it's very important to take a high-potency multiple vitamin to avoid nutrient depletion. Equally important is to check your iron levels. If you choose to continue taking BCP, avoid Saint-John's-wort, which has been shown in several studies to lower the effectiveness of BCP.

Eating Disorders: Bulimia and Anorexia

Eating disorders are common among patients with depression. With bulimia, bouts of extreme overeating are followed by depression and self-induced vomiting, purging, or fasting. With anorexia, symptoms are similar, and a person does not eat enough to maintain a healthy weight.

About 95 percent of eating disorder sufferers are female. If you are currently dealing with an eating disorder, then it may be difficult for you to follow the dietary recommendations found earlier in this book, for attempts to modify food may be a depressive trigger. My work and experience with eating disorder patients has taught me that even if patients have been recovered for years, a sudden food change can bring back old memories and tendencies. As a physician, I tread carefully in this territory.

Blood sugar balance is key when working with eating disorder issues. The steep blood sugar changes that accompany bulimia and anorexia spark depressive episodes—and these episodes continue a vicious cycle of poor eating patterns.

For blood sugar support in cases of anorexia and bulimia, I recommend the following actions in addition to the lifestyle and nutrient recommendations in this book:

- Eat a nutrient-dense breakfast to help balance blood sugar

- Eat small frequent meals, up to five small meals a day. Eating as soon as you feel hungry.

- Alternate gentle strength training and cardiovascular exercise six days a week.

- Take 400 mcg of supplemental chromium every day with food.

A few more supplements may be beneficial for alleviating both your mood and the eating disorder. Women with bulimia who were given tryptophan and vitamin B_6 throughout the day reported improvement in eating behavior, feelings about eating, and mood. It has been observed that both zinc and folate deficiency contribute to depressive symptoms in bulimia, and zinc replacement has promoted increased food intake and weight gain in anorexia patients. About half of patients with eating disorders have evidence of these nutrient deficiencies. Please add to your regimen:

- L-tryptophan: 1,000 mg three times a day

- Vitamin B_6 (pyridoxine): 45 mg three times a day

- Zinc: 30 mg twice a day, with a meal

- Folate (methylfolate form): 1,000 mcg a day

Premenstrual Syndrome and Premenstrual Dysphoric Disorder

For many women, there's a clear association between the menstrual cycle and depressed mood. Premenstrual syndrome (PMS) refers to a myriad of emotional and physical symptoms that show up five to eleven days before starting a monthly menstrual cycle. The most common physical symptoms include gas and bloating, tender breasts, clumsiness, headaches, constipation or diarrhea, and food cravings (anyone crave chocolate?). For the person with a tendency to be depressed, this time also brings on great fatigue, sad and hopeless feelings, anxiety, low libido, mood swings, trouble sleeping, and low self-esteem. Do these symptoms sound familiar?

Premenstrual dysphoric disorder (PMDD) is a similar condition, but a woman has much more severe depression symptoms, with irritability and tension before menstruation.

My short list below is very helpful in improving mood symptoms around PMS and PMDD. Please note that it's still important to read chapters 2 through 6 and start working on the bigger picture factors that could be affecting your mood.

- Exercise. Running three miles three days a week can severely decrease symptoms.

- Remove sugary foods and other refined carbohydrates from your diet. Instead, eat whole grains. Avoid removing all grains, for sometimes that can create a temporary drop in serotonin, increasing mood symptoms. Add one or two cups of liver-supportive foods (like carrots, beets, dandelion, parsnips, and kale) to your diet every day to help your liver metabolize hormones. Also, add two tablespoons of flax meal every day, for fiber is also a key to helping your liver flush excess hormones.

- Have your thyroid checked. Some studies suggest low thyroid hormone plays an especially strong role in PMS and PMDD.

- Have your iron and ferritin checked. In many menstruating female patients with depression, serum iron is normal and ferritin is low. Supplement if needed.

- Supplement your diet with any of the following:
  - Magnesium glycinate: 250 mg a day
  - Vitamin B$_6$: 50 mg a day
  - Evening primrose oil: 3 g a day
  - Crocus: 15 mg twice a day (This may be especially useful for patients with digestive symptoms [see chapter 5].)
  - L-tryptophan: 2 g three times a day from ovulation to the third day of menstruation
  - Progesterone: If the above supplements do not help after three consecutive cycles, then consider a progesterone cream from ovulation until menstruation. Follow the directions on the label. Stronger progesterone preparations are available as vaginal or rectal suppositories and through compounding pharmacists. The idea here is that in cases where there's too much circulating estrogen, progesterone can help balance it and alleviate symptoms. This seems to work well in my patients who have a strong anxiety component with PMS or PMDD, for progesterone can enhance gamma aminobutyric acid (GABA) in the brain, which is calming. In fact, some of my patients use it for relaxation before sleep. In a small percentage of patients, progesterone may increase low mood, so if you try it and your mood worsens, discontinue the progesterone.

Peri- and Postmenopausal Depression

There's a greatly expanding body of research showing the relationship between menopause and mood. One 2006 study found menopausal women were twice as likely to experience significant depressive symptoms as premenopausal women. The risk for depression onset was an astounding fourteen times higher for the twenty-four months surrounding a woman's final menses than for all the previous thirty-plus premenopausal years.

Perimenopause occurs in women between the ages of forty and fifty-five and is a time when hormones fluctuate and menstrual patterns become irregular. Menopause is the time after which the menstrual cycle completely stops.

While the risk for depression is greatest around perimenopause and menopause, the time after menopause is also a risk due to very low levels of estrogen. Currently, women can expect to live until their mid-eighties, suggesting that one-third of their lives will be spent in the postmenopausal state. As a result, we will be seeing more postmenopausal depression, too. Melatonin and Saint-John's-wort can both be beneficial for women experiencing depression during any of the three stages of menopause.

Melatonin is especially helpful with postmenopausal depression and anxiety. Many women in this situation have a delayed sleep onset and offset, meaning that their melatonin levels rise too late in the evening and then come down too late in the morning. In contrast, it has been shown that women who are morning types and like to get up soon after the sunrise tend to have more morning light exposure, which suppresses melatonin secretion during the day and results in less depressed mood. If you are peri- or postmenopausal and are having trouble getting to bed at night, and waking up in the morning, refer to the "Retraining Your Circadian Rhythm" section in chapter 5. Generally, I recommend 1 to 3 mg of melatonin thirty minutes before bedtime, with a bedtime between ten thirty and eleven p.m.

In addition to Saint-John's-wort's amazing efficacy for mild and moderate depression (see chapter 5), Saint-John's-wort may also be the therapy of choice for peri- and postmenopausal hot flashes. Women of an average age of fifty with menopausal symptoms found that after eight weeks taking Saint-John's-wort, their hot flashes decreased in duration and severity over women who took placebo. Another study showed that after three months taking Saint-John's-wort, women also reported significantly better quality of life and drastically fewer sleep problems. I like to use Saint-John's-wort with black cohosh, another herb known to help with both menopausal symptoms and low mood. Saint-John's-wort is dosed at 0.25 mg of hypericin content and 1 mg of triterpene glycosides from black cohosh twice a day. This combination has been used by botanical herbalists for decades, and these doses are supported by large-scale research as well.

Hormones and Hormone Replacement

In this section, I will discuss hormonal therapies to support your system. You may be asking yourself: Are these hormones safe for me? Or maybe: How can I get a doctor to prescribe me some hormones as soon as possible? We will answer these questions. Although hormone therapy may seem like an easy fix, I strongly encourage you to first read chapters 2 through 6 and implement the recommended diet, lifestyle, and nutrient changes as well as therapeutic modalities. It's definitely true that lowered estrogen can play a strong role in declining mood during peri- and postmenopause. However, it's important to keep in mind that many women do not have low estrogen and still experience low mood. Likewise, many women in lower estrogen states do not have low mood or depression during or after menopause.

This tells us there are a number of factors that alter the interplay between mood and hormones. I have found with my patients, the naturopathic changes recommended earlier in this book are often enough to help the body adjust to the new lower estrogen levels.

At least once a week, my office receives a call from a prospective patient who has just read one of Suzanne Somers's books and would like to start hormone replacement. Suzanne Somers is inspirational and her informative books have certainly increased awareness for many natural treatment modalities that women and men would otherwise not have heard about. I praise her for the courage to put out this information. My concern, however, is that you may read her book, or even the following hormone section, and think, I just need hormones, and then forget about everything else in this book.

Good holistic care does not simply give hormones, the same way I would not just hand you a bottle of drugs and wish you good luck. Good care looks at underlying causes and uses multiple, gentle ways to help the body heal itself. This is why all the other methods in this book need to be implemented first. In my experience, about eight out of ten women who are interested in bioidentical hormone replacement therapy end up not needing it because diet, lifestyle, stress reduction, and proper nutrients do the trick.

Okay, now that you've read my disclaimer, let's talk about hormones.

The balance of hormones affects not only the chances of getting depressed but also whether a treatment will help with peri- and postmenopausal symptoms. One research group looking at depression risk during this time of life showed an association between increased hormones for follicle stimulation (FSH) and luteinizing (LH) and jump in estrogen and FSH levels. FSH is typically low (under 20) and steady in younger, menstruating women. It rises as women enter menopause.

Rising FSH levels are not a negative event, just as menopause is not a disease state—despite what conventional medicine may have you think. This is a time when women start moving forward with creativity and newfound wisdom, and rising FSH may be responsible for it. I see many women take on painting or other arts and flourish during this time. Do you have a wise and intuitive senior female in your life? Have you sensed this intuition in yourself? If you have, do not discount it. It's very real. Of course, this can also be a time of mood swings, especially when a woman is not able or allowed to do the creative things her body and mind are naturally moving toward.

As you read this, you may want to consider the creative endeavors you have always wanted to do that you have not been able to up to this point. As Dr. Christiane Northrup reminds us in her book *Women's Bodies, Women's Wisdom*: "Now is the time when she grieves the loss of any unrealized dreams she may have had when she was a young woman, and prepares the soil for the next stage of her life."

With menopause and changing hormones, past psychological and spiritual issues need resolution as a new plan to fulfill dreams is created. It's understandable how all this can push previously happy people to be not so happy—especially if they feel like they cannot cultivate the soil.

During this time while you consider hormone replacement and the other steps in this book, please ask yourself:

- What past issues need resolution and healing? What needs to be let go? What is my plan to let go of these?

- What present issues need healing? What path do I see to work on these?

- What are my dreams and goals for the future, and what steps are needed to move toward these goals?

Hormone Replacement

While emotional and spiritual issues are a major factor in menopausal mood changes, let's switch gears to talk more about the physical side of this subject. In the medical community, low estrogen is considered a major culprit in mood issues, hot flashes, osteoporosis (bone loss), and vaginal dryness. Estrogen is known to enhance serotonin and brain-derived neurotrophic factor (BDNF), which can help elevate mood and maintain brain pathways. A number of studies have shown the benefit of giving estrogen for mood. In some women being treated for depression, estrogen replacement therapy may actually improve the effects of conventional antidepressants as well.

Unfortunately, we have learned that hormone replacement therapy (HRT) is not all that safe. In 2002, the Women's Health Initiative revealed that while reducing risk of colorectal cancer and bone fractures (which is good), HRT unfortunately increases risk of heart attack, stroke, blood clots, and breast cancer. It seems the risks of these synthetic hormones outweighs the benefits to the point that use of these commonly prescribed hormones was dramatically cut. After this study, most physicians stopped prescribing HRT, resulting in a drop in breast cancer cases estimated at fourteen thousand women per year. This was the first time breast cancer rates have ever dropped. A follow-up study in 2009 showed that ovarian cancer rates dropped 20 to 40 percent since the reduced use of HRT as well.

Bioidentical Hormones—Are These Any Safer?

While conventional medicine uses synthetic oral forms of hormones, the holistic and natural medicine world tends to use transdermal (absorbed through the skin) and vaginal (absorbed through the lining of the vagina) preparations. These are called bioidentical hormones, for they are identical to the molecules a woman has in her body.

One advantage transdermal bio identical hormones have over oral forms is that the oral forms of hormones pass through the intestinal system and go directly into the liver. The liver tries its best to sop up all the extra hormone by throwing out a lot of sex hormone binding globulin (SHBG), a protein that not only binds up estrogen and progesterone but can also tie up many other hormones, like thyroid hormones. So, in an effort to raise estrogen, oral forms of hormones can mess up thyroid function, contributing to low mood. Transdermal applications of hormones, however, seem to bother the liver much less, for the liver does not see it all come by at the same time.

Limited studies of HRT and bioidenticals have shown

- Estrogen used alone (whether natural or synthetic) increases breast cancer rate by 10 percent.
- Estrogen used with progestin (synthetic progesterone) increases breast cancer risk by 40 percent but protects the uterus from cancer.

- Estrogen used with natural micronized progesterone decreases breast cancer risk by 10 percent.

- Ovarian cancer risk seems about 40 percent higher with any hormonal replacement, natural or synthetic, oral or transdermal.

If you are considering using hormone replacement, you and your doctor need to consider your personal risks for cancer. Then think about whether you have already tried all the other natural suggestions in this book. If you have done all you can, then bio-identical hormones may be a reasonable next step.

Prescribing Natural and Bioidentical Hormones

If you have decided hormones may be worth a try, you might be wondering how to get them. To determine which hormones and the best forms you need, visit your naturopathic physician or other like-minded doctor, who can run the proper tests. Have your doctor check your current levels of estrogen, progesterone, testosterone, DHEA, DHEA sulfate, SHBG, and possibly a few others, depending on what your doctor thinks is appropriate.

The tests you need are

- Serum blood test: Your blood is tested for hormone levels.

- Salivary hormones test: You soak a cotton-type sponge with your saliva and send it to the laboratory for analysis.

- Urine hormones test: This test requires you to collect your urine for twenty-four hours. It may be the most accurate of all the tests, for it analyzes the sum of hormones that can vary from minute to minute throughout the day. While the saliva and blood tests catch a moment in time, the urine test looks at the whole day.

No single test can tell you everything, and because hormones are so complicated, I believe it's better to run all three of these tests to obtain the most accurate picture. As an aside, any doctor who tells you that she understands women's hormones and what you need is partially lying—no one fully understands this complicated system. The best thing to do is test what you can, look at your symptoms, and then make the best decision possible.

Based on the test results, your doctor may prescribe a transdermal cream with natural estrogens in three forms (estrone, bi-est, and tri-est), testosterone, DHEA, and natural progesterone. My strong advice is to ask the doctor for the lowest doses available of the hormones, monitor how you feel, and retest in one to two months. If your mood does not improve, you can slowly increase one or more of the hormones as indicated by your symptoms and the blood tests. You can visit my website www.drpeterbongiorno.com/happyhormones for a list of symptom changes with hormone use.

The overall key while using bioidenticals is to first start the naturopathic suggestions outlined in the other parts of this book, to work closely with your doctor, start slowly using the lowest doses possible, test regularly, and most importantly, see how you feel.

FOR SENIORS

As we age, life can throw out surprises and threats that can affect our mood. In my senior patients, though, I have witnessed an amazing amount of wisdom, courage, and perception that I just do not see in my younger patients. Overall, the strength and resilience in older people is inspirational. Given the trials, tribulations, and difficulties associated with aging, seniors are actually quite equipped to accommodate age-related losses and have shown that in a number of studies. I have seen natural medicines play a role in helping this process.

Any doctor working with seniors should know that this population is less likely to respond to drugs, which already have a paltry 30 percent response rate. Furthermore, more than 60 percent of patients over sixty-five experience moderate or major side effects with first-time antidepressant prescriptions.

But there's some good news: the fact is that seniors actually suffer from depression less than younger people do. One large U.S. study tells us that only 10 to 13 percent of seniors experience depression, while 18.8 percent of people younger than sixty years of age do. Also, among seniors experiencing depression, only about 5 to 10 percent of them had their first episode of depression after the age of sixty. That means that people who have not had depression earlier in life are not likely to get it after age sixty.

Senior Symptoms

If you are a senior and are experiencing low mood or are interested in supporting a senior you know, it is important to keep in mind that the experience of depression and its symptoms will vary for seniors versus that experience in a younger person. As a result, depression in older people might not parallel the strict definition for depression diagnosis and often is not expressed with sadness. Think about the typical curmudgeonly old man. Maybe it's you reading this book. This behavior is more likely a symptom of depression than a personality trait. Common symptoms of depression in seniors include

- Bodily aches and pains
- Memory problems or dementia
- Irritability and agitation
- Hypochondria
- Grumpiness and meanness
- Feeling obsolete
- Unwillingness to adapt to situations
- Talking about expecting death

Factors in Senior Depression

My experience with patients has taught me that life circumstances, including living situations, life changes, health challenges, and finances play a major role in senior mood. Understanding these and identifying the specific triggers for mood change can help patients and doctors focus on creating a plan of action.

Living Situations

Living situations can help predict who is more likely to get depressed. People over age sixty who live in communities show a depression rate of 1 to 4 percent, which is low for any population. Elderly people in primary care settings who live at home report a 6 to 9 percent depression rate. Hospitalized senior patients have up to 12 percent prevalence, and residents of long-term care facilities show a 12 to 20 percent rate of depression. One lesson from this is that it's best to stay healthy and avoid hospitalization and long-term care when possible for best mood.

Psychosocial Factors

There are a number of psychosocial factors that may contribute to the onset of senior depression. Low mood may come on with life events such as serious illness, widowhood, entering a nursing home, death or illness of close friends, loss of meaning derived from personal goals and actions, and loss of resources (money, perceived lifetime left, cognitive functioning, or social support).

Retirement, Gender, and Finances

Studies on the effect of retirement vary greatly. While some studies show that seniors are happier because they no longer work, others show no change, or worsening mood. So whether retirement is beneficial for mood is case by case. I have recommended that some of my patients look for part-time work, which seems to have helped their mood. Couples who retire at different times bring in an added dimension—retired men whose wives are still working are likely to be the least depressed while working men whose wives have retired are often the most depressed. Among couples, financial issues in retirement are more important to men, while the quality of the marital relationship is more important to women.

Religion

Interestingly, researchers examined eighty-seven depressed elderly patients, about half of whom were receiving psychotherapy, antidepressants, or a combination of the two. The best predictor of improvement in this evaluation was not these remedies but instead the "religiosity" of the patient. This gives us a sense that the more people include some type of religion in their life, the more resistant they are to depression.

CLINICAL CASE: THE DEPRESSED SENIOR

"Sylvia" was one of my first senior patients who presented with depression. Sylvia came in because her very caring primary care medical doctor had seen her emotional well-being deteriorate over the past few years and wanted her to start an antidepressant to halt the downward spiral. Sylvia was a fit seventy-five-year-old who was not interested in taking any medications—even her MD daughter could not convince her to start the medications.

Over the next six months, we discussed the difficulties Sylvia experienced in caring for both her sick husband and their mentally challenged fifty-year-old son. We also lamented about her social isolation of not seeing friends who had either moved away from the city or passed on. "Things are not the same. Things can never be the same," she repeated, thinking about the years of her young family and her place as the social center and matriarch.

We tried a base of a multiple vitamin and fish oil, plus a number of rotating supplements: SAMe, Saint-John's-wort, 5-HTP, and regular acupuncture. The acupuncture seemed to help the most in the beginning, but its effects trailed off within a few weeks. With every acupuncture treatment, we would talk about the challenges in her life along with the positive aspects. We rotated the supplements because Sylvia would become paranoid of a side effect that would cause her to take vastly lower doses than recommended, and then discontinue entirely. She didn't give any of them a chance to work.

About a year later, I received an email from Sylvia's daughter. It said: "Just want to let you know that my mom started Lexapro yesterday. We went to see her therapist together, then (her cardiologist), and she finally agreed to try medication, low dose along with some of the supplements. I think that yesterday she started to do that! Thanks for your help with her." Sylvia went on to do quite well after that.

My point with sharing this story is that whether natural or conventional treatments help is not the main factor. What is most important to remember is that the power for you, or any person, to fully heal still resides with intention and starts with a positive belief system.

Natural Support for Seniors with Depression

While the information found earlier in this book can be applied to the senior population, the following research should also be considered for specific treatment of depression in older patients.

Water

Adequate water intake may also play a role in moods of the elderly. PET imaging of older people's brains found that the midcingulate cortex can stop working prematurely and halt the body's thirst mechanism even though their bodies need more water. This discovery helps explain why the elderly are often easily dehydrated. Water is essential for transporting tryptophan into the brain for proper serotonin levels. If you are over sixty years old (or any age), it's important to drink plenty of water.

Homocysteine

A known factor in cardiovascular disease, high levels of homocysteine may also play a role in depression with aging. Checking for high blood levels and using the recommendations in chapter 4 may be helpful for the aging senior who is depressed.

Vitamin D

Selected populations may be especially prone to low vitamin D. These include the elderly, who have an increased incidence of low vitamin D. More about vitamin D is in chapter 4.

Too Little Magnesium and Too Much Calcium

Low magnesium is seen particularly often in the geriatric population, and high calcium and low magnesium intakes are associated with depression. One study checked the relationship between depression and these two minerals and found that the calcium-to-magnesium ratio in the spinal fluid and blood was elevated in depressed patients compared with non-depressed controls. Some literature suggests that higher levels of calcium may create a magnesium deficiency and that magnesium should be supplemented in these cases. Given that concerns about osteoporosis in elderly often influence doctors to pummel patients with extra calcium and vitamin D (which increases calcium absorption), plenty of magnesium should also be included for balanced mood. See chapter 5 for more about magnesium.

Acetyl-L-Carnitine

We talked about the benefits of L-carnitine for mood and energy in chapter 4. Acetyl-L carnitine is a form of carnitine that can help boost energy in the brain by acting like a neurotransmitter called acetylcholine. As such, acetyl-L-carnitine is useful for patients with depression, especially senior patients.

Acetyl-L-Carnitine Dosage and Toxicity

The supplemented dose used in most studies ranges from 1 to 3 g per day. There are no known toxicities with acetyl-L-carnitine. Mild gastrointestinal upset and vomiting were noticed in a small number of patients.

Massage

Clinically, massage has demonstrated benefits by lowering anxiety levels in the elderly.

Qi Gong and Tai Qi

One trial of qi gong therapy in seniors had two groups do ten minutes of qi gong once a day. This group exhibited reductions in anxiety, depression, fatigue, pain, and blood pressure compared to the placebo group. This was pretty exceptional for such a minimal time commitment. More about qi gong is found in chapter 6.

Even more helpful may be the ancient Chinese practice of tai qi, which combines slow movement, deep breathing, and meditation. A study in the *American Journal of Geriatric Psychiatry* looked at seventy-two depressed seniors, many of whom had been struggling with the illness for years. Treated with Lexapro, but still depressed, they were given either a two-hour tai qi class or a two-hour health education class, which included ten minutes of simple stretching exercises. After ten weeks, 94 percent of depressed older adults taking tai qi improved substantially and for 65 percent, the depression was gone. The health education group reported a 77 percent improvement, with 51 percent relapse. Importantly, the tai qi group had better physical function, memory, and thinking. Tai qi lowered inflammation, which verifies research showing tai qi helping arthritis and fibromyalgia. I believe the improvement in both groups is related to the social interaction aspect, which is very important for people wanting to heal their body.

Ginkgo Biloba

Although gingko may benefit any adult, I find one of its strongest uses is in the senior population, especially when mood change comes from cardiovascular and heart problems, a condition known as vascular depression. This type of depression occurs principally in the elderly and is caused by acute or chronic damage to the artery system in the brain. A trial of four hundred patients with dementia and mood problems gave participants either a daily dose of 240 mg of ginkgo biloba extract EGb 761 (a special well-studied version of ginkgo) or a placebo for twenty-two weeks. Ginkgo improved thinking and cognitive performance testing and alleviated feelings of apathy or indifference, anxiety, irritability, depression, sleep problems, and nighttime behavior issues. That's pretty good for a little herb.

Ginkgo has also been shown to help with the common sexual side effects that can accompany antidepressants. Please see chapter 7 for more about that.

Ginkgo Dosage and Toxicity

Ginkgo biloba extract is dosed from 40 to 80 mg three times a day, using standardized 24 percent ginkgo flavonglycosides. Ginkgo biloba leaf extract is quite low in toxicity. Forty-four trials of nearly ten thousand people showed only thirty-four cases of mild discomfort of the gastrointestinal tract, headache, or dizziness. In contrast, if you see a ginkgo tree, please remember that the ginkgo fruit pulp, which is not used to make medicine, should be avoided— severe allergic reaction and gastrointestinal irritation can result if ingested. There are many ginkgo trees lining the streets of New York City, so I see these fruits in the fall. It's interesting, for they have a strong aroma to them that almost says, "Stay away," while the leaf is beautiful and inviting to look at. Nature has a way of explaining things to us if we pay attention.

Although minimal, some research suggests ginkgo should be avoided with anticoagulants and blood thinners, diabetes medications, and when taking epilepsy drugs.

Ginkgo Plant Spirit

Ginkgo is an amazing plant with great hardiness and vitality. It was the first plant to grow back after the bombing of Hiroshima and Nagasaki. For many patients, I find it can offer a sense of strength and stability after sustaining heavy stress and feeling "bombed out." If this describes you—you may want to try some for yourself.

Green Tea (*Camellia sinensis*)

Green tea (*Camellia sinensis*) is known for having a variety of beneficial effects as an antioxidant, anti-inflammatory, and stress reducer. It is said that monks drink green tea for its ability to help with meditation by giving a calm wakefulness. It contains theanine, a calming amino acid. Frequent consumption of green tea is associated with a lower prevalence of depressive symptoms in the elderly population, according to the results of a Japanese cross-sectional study of 1,058 people.

If you are new to green tea, I recommend trying the Genmai-cha version, which combines the tea with delicious toasted rice. Some people also enjoy jasmine green tea because the dried green tea leaves are infused with the aroma of jasmine, which tricks the brain into tasting a slightly sweet flavor. Three cups of green tea a day is a reasonable dosage. Although green tea is far lower in caffeine than coffee is, people who are sensitive to caffeine may have trouble sleeping after drinking green tea.

HOW COME THEY'RE HAPPY AND I'M NOT?

Individualized Recommendation Checklist

This is a quick guide to help you keep track of which suggestions you will be using for lifting your mood. It is important to remain consistent with your food, lifestyle, and supplement additions. Mark the suggestions that fit your specific needs best; then check back to this list once a week to make sure you are following everything as best as you can. Going forward, you may want to make changes to the plan. Using this checklist should help you keep it sorted out.

NUTRITION

❑ Eat breakfast with protein every morning.

❑ Snack and eat small meals throughout the day.

❑ Drink 60 ounces of water each day.

❑ Eat about 0.5 g protein for every pound you weigh every day.

❑ Eat one cup of raw nuts and seeds each day.

❑ Eat fish three times a week.

❑ Eat one cup of green vegetables or two celery ribs every day.

❑ Eat one fruit a day.

- ❏ Pomegranate (1/2 to one whole fruit a day or 3 ounces of juice)
- ❏ Incorporate more beans into your diet.
- ❏ Drink two to four cups of coffee each day (without sugar)—unless you have anxiety or insomnia.
- ❏ Add crunchy health foods to your diet: for example, celery, raw nuts and seeds, baby carrots, fiber crackers, and dried vegetables.

SLEEP

- ❏ Get at least eight hours of sleep each night, with a bedtime by eleven p.m.
- ❏ If you have trouble falling asleep or staying asleep, try
    - ❏ Creating a calming evening ritual
    - ❏ Banning bright light a half hour before bed
    - ❏ Taking melatonin: regular 1–9 mg a half hour before bed to fall asleep, or the time-released version to fall asleep and stay asleep (3–9 mg)
    - ❏ Taking tryptophan: 1,000 mg
    - ❏ Taking valerian or passion flower
    - ❏ Taking motherwort
    - ❏ Using light box therapy: in the morning for seasonal affective disorder
    - ❏ Taking adrenal support: in the morning for helping to reset sleep rhythm

EXERCISE

Move your body every day at whatever level is possible for you. Try for a minimum of twenty-five minutes walking three times a week, preferably in the morning sunlight.

CONTRAST HYDROTHERAPY

Take a shower at a comfortable warm temperature and slowly cool down the water over a five-minute period to 68 degrees Fahrenheit, at which point you can sustain for two to three minutes. This may be especially effective for patients who have responded well to Cymbalta or other SNRI medications.

SUNLIGHT

Spend some time in the sunshine every day, preferably in the morning.

LIFESTYLE/WORK

- ❏ Avoid TV.
- ❏ Avoid smoking, alcohol, and MSG.

BRING IN THE NEW

- ❏ Positivity Work
- ❏ Psychotherapy
- ❏ Cognitive Behavioral Therapy
- ❏ Interpersonal Therapy
- ❏ Yoga
- ❏ Massage
- ❏ Meditation and Breathing: for those with excess anxiety and restlessness
- ❏ Qi Gong: for depressed individuals who tend to stay inside and not move much
- ❏ Religious or Spirituality Practice
- ❏ Acupuncture and Traditional Chinese Medicine
- ❏ Manipulation Work

- [ ] Craniosacral Therapy
- [ ] Emotional Freedom Technique
- [ ] Biofeedback
- [ ] Art Therapy
- [ ] Music Therapy

GENERAL SUPPLEMENTATION

- [ ] Fish oil: containing at least 1,000 mg of EPA per day
- [ ] High-potency multiple vitamin
- [ ] Vitamin D: 4,000 IU a day if you do not know your level. Take more if needed based on blood tests.

SPECIFIC SUPPLEMENTATION

Supplements for antidepressant medications that are not working well:

- [ ] Methyl-folate (folic acid): 15 mg a day
- [ ] Zinc: 25 mg a day with food
- [ ] Vitamin B_{12}: 1 mg a day
- [ ] Hormonal supports
- [ ] Testosterone
- [ ] Thyroid support and replacement

Supplements for medications causing sexual side effects:

- [ ] Ginkgo biloba: 40 to 80 mg of extract three times a day
- [ ] Yohimbine: work with a practitioner

Supplements to help wean off medications (work with your prescribing doctor for this):

- [ ] 5HTP: for SSRIs, SNRIs, and tricyclic antidepressants
- [ ] Tryptophan: for SSRIs and SNRIs

- ❏ Saint-John's-wort: for SSRIs
- ❏ Tyrosine: for SNRIs and tricyclic antidepressants
- ❏ Ginkgo biloba: for tricyclic antidepressants
- ❏ Mucuna: for bupropion and aripiprazole

Supplements for sugar craving or if your blood sugar is too high or low:

- ❏ Chromium: 400 mcg per day with food
- ❏ Cinnamon: ½ tsp a day

Supplements for constipation:

- ❏ Fiber supplement like psyllium, flax meal, or other

Supplements to build neurotransmitters:

- ❏ Vitamin B_6 or pyridoxal 5-phosphate: 50 mg a day
- ❏ Magnesium: 200 to 600 mg a day
- ❏ Tryptophan: 500 to 2,000 mg a day in divided doses
- ❏ 5-HTP: Up to 200 mg three times a day
- ❏ SAMe: Ramp up to 400 mg four times a day, best effect in people over fifty years old

Supplements for increasing motivation:

- ❏ D-phenylalanine: up to 350 mg a day
- ❏ Tyrosine: 500 to 1,000 mg up to three times a day

Supplements for stress management:

- ❏ Phosphatidylserine: 200 to 800 mg a day in divided doses

Herbal choices:

- ❏ Saint-John's-wort: 900 to 1,800 mg a day in divided doses; best for chronic low mood without incapacitating depression

- ❏ Lavender: For excess aggression or anxiety; can take orally or as an aroma therapy
- ❏ Rhodiola: 340 to 1,000 mg a day for low self-esteem and adrenal fatigue
- ❏ Crocus (saffron): 15 mg for depression with digestive issues
- ❏ Sage: For help processing buried issues that prevent moving on in life; burn in smudging ceremony

Homeopathics:

- ❏ Arsenicum album: perfectionistic and anxious
- ❏ Aurum metallicum: serious, despair, possibly suicidal
- ❏ Calcarea carbonica: childlike, teary, menstrual-related low mood
- ❏ Causticum: lot of loss experienced, crying, feels injustice
- ❏ Cimicifuga: headaches, swings of energy and depression, exaggerated fears
- ❏ Ignatia amara: grief from loss, lump in throat, keeps hurt inside
- ❏ Kali phosphoricum: insomnia, indigestion, exhaustion, and nervousness
- ❏ Natrum carbonicum: depression is experienced after a hurt, disappointment, or illness
- ❏ Natrum muriaticum: private and reserved person, cries alone, inadequate parent bonding
- ❏ Natrum sulphuricum: depression and mood changes post-head injury
- ❏ Phosphoricum Acidum: gray hair after stressor, fatigued, drained, low motivation
- ❏ Pulsatilla: looks for consolation, childlike, loves fresh air
- ❏ Sepia: great fatigue, slow digestion, organ prolapse

❏ Staphysagria: depression from anger or suppressed emotion, easily offended

Please see chapter 5 for more remedy specifics.

BLOOD WORK

Refer to the blood test list in chapter 4 and schedule appropriate tests with to your doctor.

Out of Range Blood Work

Low cholesterol/low HDL:

❏ Add oranges, dark chocolate, extra virgin olive oil, and hibiscus and black teas to your diet.

❏ Add 6 g of beta-glucan fiber supplement or oat bran.

❏ Consider stopping statin medication (with prescribing doctor's help) to see if this helps mood.

High homocysteine:

❏ SAMe: 400 mg four times a day

❏ B-complex vitamin every day

❏ Betaine: 3,600 mg a day

High CRP:

❏ Exercise

❏ Minimize highly cooked food

❏ Psyllium husk: 1 teaspoon twice a day in a big glass of water, plus plenty of fruits and vegetables

❏ Vitamin C: 500 mg three times a day

❏ Vitamin E: Mixed tocopherols 1,200 IU a day

Low serum ferritin:

❏ Iron: 25 mg up to three times a day with food

Low thyroid function:

❏ Seaweed and kelp
❏ Thyroid glandular support
❏ Selenium: 200 mcg a day
❏ Tyrosine: 300 mg a day
❏ Consider natural thyroid replacement (Armour Thyroid, Nature-Throid) or T3 (Cytomel)

Low DHEA:

❏ DHEA: 5 to 15 mg a day, higher if needed

Low testosterone:

❏ Testosterone patch or compound pharmacy testosterone cream

Positive celiac panel:

❏ Avoid all wheat and gluten sources

Low serum carnitine:

❏ L-carnitine: 500 mg twice a day on an empty stomach

Low folic acid or B$_{12}$:

❏ Folic acid: 800 mcg of methyltetrahydrofolate form every day
❏ Vitamin B$_{12}$: 1 mg every day; more may be needed if you are taking medications that are not working

Low vitamin D:

❏ Vitamin D: 2,000 IU with food per day for every 10 ng/dL below 50 ng/dL

DETOXIFY

❑ Learn your blood type and consider following the dietary plan outlined in chapter 3.

❑ Lower exposures to heavy metals, pesticides, and chemicals in household cleaners, lotions, and so on.

❑ Follow steps 1, 2, and 3 of the detoxification plan in chapter 4.

SPECIFICALLY FOR WOMEN

If on birth control pills:

❑ Multivitamin

❑ Extra B-complex vitamins

❑ Do not take Saint-John's-wort

If dealing with an eating disorder:

❑ Eat a nutritious breakfast and small, frequent meals

❑ Gentle exercise every day

❑ Chromium: 400 mcg a day

❑ L-tryptophan: 1,000 mg three times a day

❑ Vitamin B_6: 45 mg every day

❑ Zinc: 30 mg twice a day

❑ Folate: 1,000 mcg once a day

PMS and Premenstrual Dysphoric Disorder (PMDD):

❑ Exercise

❑ Remove carbs and add flax meal and a liver food (like beets or kale)

❑ Check thyroid and iron levels

❑ Add the following supplements:

    ❑ Magnesium glycinate: 250 mg a day

- ❏ Vitamin B$_6$: 50 mg a day
- ❏ Evening primrose oil: 3 g a day
- ❏ Crocus: 15 mg twice a day
- ❏ Tryptophan: 2 g three times a day from ovulation to the third day of menstruation
- ❏ Progesterone: dosed on the label from ovulation until menstruation; discontinue if mood worsens

Peri- and Post menopausal depression:

- ❏ Consider increasing soy intake and flax meal
- ❏ Melatonin: 1 to 3 mg before bed
- ❏ Saint-John's-wort and black cohosh combined: 0.25 mg of hypericin content of Saint-John's-wort and 1 mg of triterpene glycosides from black cohosh twice a day
- ❏ Consider bioidentical hormonal replacement

SPECIFICALLY FOR SENIORS

- ❏ Drink adequate water
- ❏ Consider a support group or religious work if it speaks to you
- ❏ Acetyl-L-carnitine: 1 to 3 g a day
- ❏ Massage
- ❏ Qi gong and tai qi
- ❏ Ginkgo biloba: 40 to 80 mg of extract three times a day
- ❏ Green tea: three cups a day

OTHER TESTS TO CONSIDER

- ❏ Heavy metal urine test
- ❏ Blood heavy metal test
- ❏ Saliva cortisol test
- ❏ Urine hormonal test

REFERENCES AND RESOURCES

This book is highly supported with the author's collection of more than sixteen years of data and peer-reviewed journal articles on the subject of depression. Please visit: www.drpeterbongiorno.com/HappyReferences for a complete listing of each chapter's references.

WHAT IS A NATUROPATHIC DOCTOR?

When I first see new patients with depression, or any other kind of chronic issue, I spend at least an hour and a half at the first visit asking lots of questions about their life. In fact, many of my patients have left this initial visit saying, "Wow, you know more about me than anyone else does." Well, it's an honor and a privilege to be so trusted. I spend time asking a lot of questions up front because patients' answers offer strong clues to what remedies may be most effective. This habit of asking all these questions in a thoughtful, complete, and relaxed manner is not my invention—I learned it when I was training as a naturopathic doctor.

Naturopathic doctors (NDs) are trained in post-college, four-year medical programs. NDs learn all the basics of primary care medicine at the same level that conventional doctors (MDs or DOs) do. NDs learn about anatomy, physiology, biochemistry, physical exams, minor surgery, blood draws, pharmacology (the study of medications), and so on. For students, the number of learning hours for NDs is equivalent to that of MDs. NDs are trained with a greater emphasis on primary care experience with patients one on one and less emphasis on hospitals and urgent care.

Another difference between the two stems from philosophy: conventional medicine focuses on a body that runs in systems, while naturopathic physicians look at the body as a whole system as much as possible. For example, when you have a skin problem, in the conventional world you would work with a dermatologist (a skin doctor). When you have an issue with your digestive tract you would see a gastroenterologist (a stomach/intestine doctor). In the naturopathic world, many skin problems can result from digestive issues, so we would work with the digestive system to help clear the skin.

To that end, the naturopathic curriculum also adds many types of classes a conventional doctor does not receive. We learn extensively about diet, lifestyle, exercise, nutrients, herbal medicines, hydrotherapy, and homeopathic medicines, and we receive plenty of classes in counseling. In fact, in my naturopathic school, students had to go to counseling too. It was explained, "In order to be present with someone else, and their challenges, you must understand your own so they do not get in the way." Have you ever met a doctor and felt like you couldn't connect? That may be because she was having a bad day or because there were issues she needed to work on herself. We all have them.

In that spirit, from day one, naturopathic students are taught to help each patient look for the underlying cause of illness. We are taught that the body has an innate ability to heal itself and that if we give the body what it needs, it can heal.

Naturopathic physicians are licensed to practice medicine in sixteen states and the District of Columbia. In those states, we practice as primary care physicians, with the responsibilities, rights, and privileges of any physicians. A few states limit the rights of drug prescribing.

I am vice president of the New York Association of Naturopathic Physicians. In our particular state, NDs are not licensed as physicians (even though our neighbor to the north, Connecticut, has been licensed since 1922), but we are actively pursuing our medical license. It seems in our state, and in many others, the societies of medical doctors would prefer we do not have a license. I think the concern is we may take away their business. Given the shortage of primary care doctors and the sense of abundance about the world, we know that there are plenty of patients—so my hope is in time, the public in all states, including the state of New York, will have the choice of seeing a naturopathic physician as their primary care doctor.

FINDING A NATUROPATHIC DOCTOR

American Association of Naturopathic Physicians
www.naturopathic.org
The American Association of Naturopathic Physicians (AANP) is the official association of credited naturopathic physicians. If you are looking to find a natural medicine expert in your area, please visit this website.

Peter Bongiorno ND, LAc
www.drpeterbongiorno.com
Dr. Bongiorno's website contains a full listing of all his publications as well as a blog where he shares his newest insights regarding the best in natural medicine health care and research. You'll also find links to his Facebook and Twitter pages. He invites you to join in the discussions.

Inner Source Natural Health and Acupuncture
www.innersourcehealth.com
This is the website for Dr. Bongiorno's clinical practice in New York, which he co-directs with his wife, Dr. Pina LoGiudice. Please sign up for their newsletter, which gives regular information about the best natural medicine and acupuncture has to offer.

OTHER ELECTRONIC RESOURCES

These are some resources I have found helpful in my journey to bring good quality information to my patients.

Please note the author receives no financial compensation from these companies.

Food and Nutrition

World's Healthiest Foods
www.whfoods.com
Possibly the single best resource to learn about the health benefits of foods. This site is noncommercial and contains medical research, recipes, and more.

Books/Relaxation Materials/Lectures

Shambhala Publications
www.shambhala.com
This publishing company is a wonderful resource for books and materials to help create keep positive messages flowing.

Cognitive Behavioral Therapy

Good Days Ahead DVD
www.helpfordepression.com/good-days-ahead
Good Days Ahead is a cognitive behavioral therapy–based DVD that uses researched methods to teach individuals coping skills for managing stress, anxiety, and depression.

Emotional Freedom

Emotional Freedom Technique
www.eftuniverse.com
Emotional Freedom Technique (EFT) is a simple healing system that reduces the stress underlying much disease. It works on a variety of health issues, psychological problems, and performance

issues, even those that have been resistant to other methods. It can be learned and applied rapidly, which has contributed to its popularity among millions of people.

Nontoxic Products

Environmental Working Group
www.ewg.org
The mission of the Environmental Working Group (EWG) is to use the power of public information to protect public health and the environment. In building what is probably one of the best noncommerical, nonbiased, factual sites regarding environment, writers have wonderfully researched lists regarding safe-to-use skin products, sunscreens, and common household items. I use this website over and over for good information about toxins and health.

Other Holistic Practitioners

The American Holistic Medical Association
www.holisticmedicine.org
This is the website for holistic medical doctors and other like-minded practitioners who are also focused on integrating holistic medicine into their practice.

National Certification Commission of Acupuncture and Oriental Medicine
www.nccaom.org
Only master's-level trained diplomates in acupuncture are found on this site. For someone using acupuncture to treat depression, it is recommended that the acupuncturist is certified by the NCCAOM as a diplomate in acupuncture.

American Board of Clinical Metal Toxicology
www.abcmt.org
This is a great resource to find physicians trained to understand how heavy metals can cause disease and how to remove these toxins.

BOOKS

On Depression

Healing Depression: Integrated Naturopathic and Conventional Treatments
Dr. Peter Bongiorno
CCNM Press, 2010
This book is written to teach physicians how to work with patients suffering from depression by using natural and integrative treatments. It's a very detailed, great source for people in the medical profession and anyone who would like to read about this information at a higher level of scientific discussion. This would also be a book to bring to your physician. This can be purchased by visiting www.drpeterbongiorno.com.

The Estrogen-Depression Connection: The Hidden Link Between Hormones & Women's Depression
Karen J. Miller, PhD, and Steven A. Rogers, PhD
New Harbinger Publications, 2007
This book is a great source for understanding in more depth how a woman's hormonal system plays a strong role in mood as well as menstrual issues, menopause, and general health.

Lifting Depression: A Neuroscientist's Hands-On Approach to Activating Your Brain's Healing Power
Kelly Lambert, PhD
Basic Books, 2008
Lambert's book is an interesting study about the importance of hands-on physical work to build a more competent mood and brain.

Manufacturing Depression: The Secret History of a Modern Disease
Gary Greenberg
Simon & Schuster, 2010
This book is a fascinating and perceptive tour of the history of depressive illness and antidepressant dominance.

On Health

What the Drug Companies Won't Tell You and Your Doctor Doesn't Want You to Know: The Alternative Treatments That May Change Your Life—and the Prescriptions That Could Harm You
Michael T. Murray, ND
Atria Books, 2009
Dr. Murray has a wonderful ability to connect dots regarding health, disease, and all the environmental, social, and economic factors that are at play when it comes to our health.

Encyclopedia of Natural Medicine
Michael Murray, ND, and Joseph Pizzorno, ND
Three Rivers Press, 1997
This is an excellent basic guide about natural medicine as well as specific treatments for a host of common conditions.

Eat Right 4 Your Type: The Individualized Diet Solution to Staying Healthy, Living Longer & Achieving Your Ideal Weight
Peter J. D'Adamo with Catherine Whitney
Putnam, 1997
This book is a landmark work in using the right foods to heal your body and to figure out which foods may be inflaming your body.

INDEX

tryptophan
  digestion and production of, 76–77
  inflammation due to impaired
    availability of, 78
  vitamins assisting conversion of, 106
  water intake benefits, 17, 208
L-tryptophan
  for antidepressant discontinuation
    support, 184
  for eating disorders, 195
  for premenstrual conditions, 197
  supplementation of, 39, 40,
    109–112, 113, 114
TSH (Thyroid Stimulating Hormone), 61
turmeric, 91
tyrosine, 112–115, 184, 185

Ullman, Dana, 131
urine tests, for heavy metals, 84

valerian, 39, 40
vascular depression, 210
vis medicatrix naturae, 15
*vitamins. See also specific names of
  vitamins*
  for amino acid conversion, 106
  for anemia/iron deficiencies, 59
  blood tests for levels of, 64, 69–71, 72
  deficiencies in, 64, 69–73, 106–107,
    209
  for depression, overview, 8, 103,
    106–107
  for eating disorders, 195
  for high CRP, 57
  for high homocysteine, 54
  for hormone production, 71
  medications depleting, 193, 194
  for medication support, 11, 173–174,
    175, 216

multiple formulas, 8–9, 42
for neurotransmitter support, 8
for premenstrual conditions, 197
purpose of, 8
quality selection, 8–9
for serotonin synthesis, 69

water, 10, 16–17, 76, 86, 208
water therapy, 138–140, 215
Wellbutrin, 40, 128, 185
withdrawal, drug, 181–182, 186–185
women
  birth control pills, 193–194, 221
  blood sugar and gender
    comparisons, 190
  blood testing and menstruation, 7
  bowel movements and self-esteem
    links, 75
  coffee intake, 22
  eating disorders, 194–195, 221
  hormonal therapies, 199–204
  marriage and divorce, 190–191
  menopause, 197–199
  premenstrual conditions, 196–197,
    221–222
  social situations and stress, 192–193
  suicide, 190
work-life balance, 15, 215
World Health Organization, 120

yellow dock, 59
yin and yang, 157
yoga, 153–155
yohimbe, 179–181

zinc, 12, 94, 107–108, 174–175, 194,
  195
Zyban, 128, 185

ABOUT THE AUTHOR

 DR. PETER BONGIORNO is a natural medicine practitioner with offices in New York City and Long Island. He is a graduate of Bastyr University, the leading accredited university for science-based natural medicine, and vice-president of the New York Association of Naturopathic Physicians. He is also a member of the American Association for Naturopathic Physicians and Physicians for Social Responsibility. Dr. Bongiorno is licensed as an acupuncturist in the State of New York and as a naturopathic doctor in the State of Washington, where naturopathic doctors are licensed to practice medicine.

Dr. Bongiorno is an adjunct faculty member at New York University, where he teaches classes on Holistic Healing, and is also on faculty at the Natural Gourmet Institute for Food and Health. Dr. Bongiorno also teaches medical students at Mount Sinai School of Medicine about natural medicine and acupuncture in its Arts and Sciences of Medicine program.

Visit him at *www.innersourcehealth.com*